MW00438896

# KANSAS CITY
# WOMEN
## OF INDEPENDENT MINDS

*Another book of interest:*

KANSAS CITY STYLE
A Social and Cultural History of Kansas City
As Seen Through Its Lost Architecture

by Dory DeAngelo and Jane Fifield Flynn

# KANSAS CITY
# WOMEN

## OF INDEPENDENT MINDS

## JANE FIFIELD FLYNN

FIFIELD PUBLISHING CO. / KANSAS CITY, MISSOURI

Fifield Publishing Co.
P.O. Box 30302
Kansas City, MO 64112

FIRST EDITION

Library of Congress Catalog Card Number 92-073297

ISBN: 0-9633758-0-6

Printed in the United States of America by
The Lowell Press, Inc., 115 East 31st Street, Kansas City, MO 64108

*To my family and friends for their
encouragement, assistance, and patience
profferred to this ofttimes cranky writer.*

# I Shall Come Singing

Oh, I shall burst this bondage with my soul,
And soar with swifter courses than the dawn;
Rising resistless as the sun, the bowl
Of heaven breaking with the beauty drawn
Out of this surging turbulence of fire,
Expanding, spreading with a dazzling light,
Shedding the radiance of deep desire
Over the shackled, dark despair of night.
I shall arise with singing, and my song
Shall be as wind upon the mountain peak;
Perhaps I may be silent overlong,
Dumb with a glory which I cannot speak,
But I shall burst this bondage, for in me
Is beauty singing skyward, free . . . free . . . free!

HELEN ROWE HENZE
*Each Man's World*
Frank Glenn Publishing Co.,
Kansas City, Missouri

# CONTENTS

# PREFACE

THE SPARK TO WRITE this book came from the realization, prompted by many years of research, that the public has not been
given an opportunity to know and appreciate the roles women have
played over the years in determining the history of Kansas City.
Their influence was broad and varied. Some helped shape policy by
participating in the political system, while others made their presence known in areas such as business, education, medicine, law,
entertainment, volunteer work, sports, and philanthropy. Some
were internationally famous, some infamous, and all had a connection to Kansas City during some period of their lives. Little refer-
ence in local publications is given to their accomplishments, yet my
poking into early materials was a revelation both in the number and
the scope of influence and importance of women. For every one
included in this book, there are at least three more waiting in the
wings . . . for, perhaps, another book? The selection process was
not an easy one. There will be glaring omissions for some readers
because of my attempt to present interesting and uncommon
careers covering a wide span of time. The easiest decision was
where to begin.

The story begins with the first white woman to come to the
area. Berenice Chouteau arrived as an 18-year-old bride in 1821 and
was confronted with all the perils of frontier life: epidemics,
plagues, and the daily fight for survival for herself and her family.
Little, if any, time was left for intellectual pursuits. Gradually, other
women settled here; many were educated. As their household and
childrearing responsibilities eased, some began to feel a restlessness,
a hunger for mental stimulation, and female companionship.

Small groups began to gather, usually in private homes. It was
from one of these informal gatherings the first "club" came into

being, the Tuesday Afternoon Class. Although intrepid, these women were not sufficiently foolhardy to use the word "club" for in 1881 it was considered much too masculine. Later that year, with Sarah Chandler Coates as its founder and first president, the class was renamed the History Club of '82. Social niceties were not part of the agenda as the club's charge was to "stimulate torpid minds." In fact, some clubs openly condemned those guilty of gossip. The members gathered for serious study as evidenced by the '82 Club's initial choice of literature: an 800-page volume, *Green's History of the English People*, followed by equally impressive tomes about the people of France and Germany. From the early clubs sprang other clubs that broadened the scopes of interest. Women managed to ignore public ridicule, which came in the form of cartoons and jokes, as they continued their study of literature, science, and the arts.

A change began to occur when they, free-born citizens and tax-payers, objected to being denied the right to vote. To remedy this, many clubs turned into bands of insurgents by saying goodbye to their loftier pursuits and deciding it was time to address their role not only for the present but also the future. Doors of the clubs were thrown open as women took to the streets to rally for the cause. Coates, an ardent suffragist, was so passionate about women's suffrage that some friends frequently crossed the street to avoid one of her lengthy discourses. Many women took to the stump, crisscrossing the state. Their efforts were rewarded when Missouri women were given the right to vote in 1920.

Flush with success they turned their attention to other civic matters. They were not bashful in publicly criticizing the men of the city for not accomplishing much in the political arena. Pooling their skills, women identified and systematically addressed community needs: schools, playgrounds, street lighting, symphony orchestra, prison reform, child welfare, fire protection, world peace, unemployment, property rights for women, art institute, birth control (the General Federation of Women's Clubs voted in favor of it in 1935), and many other concerns. Women acted as leaders and workers in ousting the Pendergast machine.

It is interesting to note that many of these women who were active in causes were housewives, financially secure to pursue their interests. Their accomplishments have been virtually ignored. In

1914 Lois Oldham Henrici, a Kansas Citian, published a book of who's who of women in America. It was the first time in the nation's history that there was a listing of women by profession. The book was published by The Crafter, a Kansas City printing business owned by Ada M. Kassimer and operated entirely by women.

Realizing that care of the body was important, the Kansas City Women's Athletic Club, only the second such club in the country, opened at 1023 Walnut Street in 1908. It was an immediate success, so much so that before the end of the first year the club moved to much larger quarters at 1015 Grand Avenue to accommodate the 600-plus members.

More and more women entered business, law, and medicine many out of a need to support themselves and their families. In 1922 the first Kansas City Businesswomen's Show was held. Sponsored by the Women's Commercial Club, the forerunner of the Women's Chamber of Commerce, the show was an eyeopener for the community. Accomplishments in business were acknowledged. Several years later another step was taken with the opening of a woman's apartment hotel at 2928 Forest Avenue that was designed by Nelle Peters.

However, women were not always accepted. In 1926 a woman was slated to join Carolyn Farwell Fuller as a member of the Kansas City Board of Education, and several male members of the board threatened to resign. Men wondered what would women try to do next. Some women were firmly convinced that they had been running things for a long time and it was time for men to admit it.

During the Depression a different question arose. Should married women, who were not dependent upon a salary, be employed instead of an unemployed man with family responsibilities? The Kansas City Council of Churches favored the unemployed husband. However, women's clubs countered that women had as much right to a job as did a man.

Another shot was fired when a prominent businessman went on record saying, "Every university and every college, offering training for women other than home life and preparation for motherhood should be padlocked. Such institutions undermine the primary purpose of women as the replacers of the human race." Charges and countercharges flew. Little was settled except to make the women fighting for equality more resolute in their efforts. Some of the women most affected by sexism were those in the business community. The Women's Chamber of Commerce was a tower of strength for it did, and still does, provide the opportunity for professionals to share experiences and be recognized for their achievements. There have been changes in these attitudes, but many women still feel sexism is practiced in subtler ways.

During the last five decades women have surged into the work force, elective offices, professional sports, and all phases of entertainment. The paths they followed were illuminated by these 92 women, to whom we owe a huge debt of gratitude.

This book is tribute to them. I hope this work can be considered a small downpayment on that debt as it recognizes Kansas City women of independent minds whose caring and diligence of purpose changed the community.

JANE FIFIELD FLYNN

# ACKNOWLEDGMENTS

IT WOULD BE infinitely more satisfying if I were able to express my appreciation to each of you individually for all your assistance in making this book possible. I took an idea, put together all the information you so generously provided, and fashioned it into this book. Many of you shared with me long-forgotten events and photographs that have made the women on these pages come alive.

The real challenge in producing *Kansas City Women of Independent Minds* was locating usable photographs. Some have come from family collections, and others were found in the safekeeping of the Jackson County Historical Society Archives; Landmarks Commission of Kansas City, Missouri; Kansas City Museum; Nelson-Atkins Museum of Art; Aurora Davis of *The Kansas City Star* library; Bruce R. Watkins Cultural Heritage Center; *The Call*; Woman's City Club; Kansas City Young Matrons; and the Photograph Collection of the University of Missouri-Kansas City. With many photographs Jack Denzer Photo Services, Inc., worked miracles to make them printable. My very special thanks to Jack, Margaret D. Lewis, and Floranne Long for their interest, patience, and expeditious processing.

For many months my home-away-from-home was the Missouri Valley Special Collections at the Kansas City Public Library. Without the willing help of department head Gloria Maxwell and Sara Hallier, Sandra Gates, Beth Whitaker, Kathryn Maciel, Alberta Francisko, and Marjorie Kinney, who recently retired, this book could not have been written.

The question of a title was answered by the creative minds of Wilda and Hal Sandy. As always, they came through.

My undying gratitude is extended to Barbara W. Funk for her editing, advising, maintaining a sense of humor, smoothing the many rough parts, and bringing it all together. Last but far from least, my deep appreciation to The Lowell Press for its impeccable craftsmanship in producing this volume.

To all the above, thank you.

JANE FIFIELD FLYNN

# KANSAS CITY
# WOMEN
## OF INDEPENDENT MINDS

# ANGIE SANDIFER AKER

I HEAR FOLKS HOLLER about the good old days. I was born 71 years ago, long enough ago to remember those days and to know I've really enjoyed my old age better than my younger days." That's not surprising when you learn Angie Sandifer Aker's story.

She was born August 26, 1911, in Crystal Springs, Mississippi, one of nine children of sharecroppers Jimmie and Anna Sandifer. They were a black family living in the segregation of the Deep South. The school for black children went only to the eighth grade and was open just three months a year because students were needed to work in the fields of cotton, corn, and vegetables. Angie Sandifer remembered watching white children pass by in covered wagons as she walked to school, which was one room of the black church. "They would stop, get out of the wagon, tease you, spit on you, hit you, throw dirt on you. This was against everything I had been taught by my family."

The family endured until Jimmie Sandifer suffered a badly crushed leg. Receiving inadequate medical attention, he was not able to plant the crops, their sole source of

COURTESY KAYCEE MOORE

*Angie Sandifer Aker*

1

income. Thus, the family fell into the very depths of poverty. It was only the strong will and hard work of her mother that saved the family. She taught her children that "if it's worth doing at all, it's worth doing good. Do it good because you will have to if you expect to have a job. Tell the truth because if you don't, you won't love yourself and nobody else will love you." Angie Sandifer's maternal grandfather, born a slave, also had a great influence on her childhood. His favorite expression, "Don't let me catch you slue footin' around," stayed with his granddaughter throughout her life.

On December 1, 1931, Angie Sandifer married Andrew Collier. In 1943 they came north to Kansas City. Collier died three years later, leaving her with a new mortgage and six children ranging in age from eight months to nine years. She took in laundry and did domestic work to support her family.

She came to know the disease that would take the lives of two of her children: sickle cell anemia, a genetic disease found chiefly among blacks. Both Angie and Andrew Collier had been carriers of the disease. While visiting one son in the hospital, she met Rufus Aker, a hospital orderly. She married him and bore three more children. In 1971, she once again was widowed, but this time she was a woman with a mission.

Angie Aker's experiences at General Hospital No. 2 had been nightmares. There was no help for families affected by sickle cell anemia. In fact, she said, "It was almost never correctly diagnosed. The pain just kept getting worse and worse and no one understood." Aker took it upon herself to change that when she founded the Kansas City Chapter for Sickle Cell, Inc., in 1976. Her goal was to educate blacks, insist on blood tests to identify carriers, improve the quality of life for those who had the disease, and help with their expenses. It was through her efforts that it became a state law that all infants born in Missouri be tested for sickle cell anemia. She remained executive director of the chapter until 1989.

Aker was an advocate for many causes, including the elderly. She became active in senior citizens' movements city- and statewide. Aker was appointed to the Governor's Advisory Council on Aging, twice attended White House conferences on aging, was a charter member of the local Gray Panthers, formed the Mid-City Chapter of the American Association of Retired Persons (AARP), was a member of the Missouri Silver-Haired Legislature, and served on the board of directors of Truman Medical Center-West and the Mid-America Regional Council. In 1976, she met President Gerald Ford at the White House and was appointed to a committee to welcome the Emperor of Japan. At the same time she was named an International Woman of the Year. All of this was accomplished by a poorly educated sharecropper's daughter.

Financially, life did not become easier. Her income consisted of a monthly $329 Social Security check.

Angie Aker, who enriched Kansas City with her hard work and "doing good," died December 22, 1990, at the age of 79.

# MAE ARBAUGH

Two Carry Nations? In a way this is true. The more familiar one toted a hatchet while crusading against alcoholic beverages and firearms in the early 1900s. The other was Mae "Carry Nation" Arbaugh, who for 31 years took mighty swings of the bat as a professional softball player.

Born in Kansas in 1884, Arbaugh grew up in a home at Independence and Tracy avenues. Very early in her life she began to be called Carry by her family and friends for reasons that remain unknown. Her professional softball teammates expanded the moniker to "Carry Nation."

Arbaugh's professional softball career began at the age of 14 when a promoter from Chicago noticed her playing with her sister Leah on a vacant lot as he rode by on a streetcar. Even though they were very young, he could spot their athletic gifts. Approaching the girls' parents, he persuaded them to allow the sisters to travel to Chicago to play professional softball. The Arbaugh girls joined the Chicago Bloomer Girls and played together for four years. Then Leah married, left the game, and returned to Kansas City.

Mae "Carry Nation" Arbaugh went on to become the star first baseman for the team and later played the same position for the Boston Bloomer Girls. According to her sister, she earned a lot of money and spent it as fast as she earned it. During off-seasons, finding herself short of funds, she worked at the Jones Dry Goods Company at Sixth and Main streets supervising a crew of painters and decorators.

One of the greatest highlights of her life was appearing with Lou Gehrig, the legendary New York Yankee baseball player, on "Ripley's Believe It Or Not" radio program. Arbaugh's claim to fame was that she had surpassed Gehrig's achievement of 2,130 career games played: she had been in 6,486. Another memorable moment occurred when she caught a ball that had been dropped from the top of the 16-story Waldheim Building at 6 Petticoat Lane.

In 1929, Arbaugh retired from playing professional softball and returned to Kansas City where she held a variety of jobs. In retirement she never lost her love for the game; she managed amateur softball teams and remained an ardent fan of the Kansas City Blues.

Mae Arbaugh died on June 20, 1941, the same year as Gehrig. She left a remarkable legacy of 31 years and over 6,000 games played as a female professional softball player.

# MARY McAFEE ATKINS

THE CORNERSTONE OF the Nelson-Atkins Museum of Art was laid 20 years after the death of one of the museum's benefactors, Mary McAfee Atkins. After William Rockhill Nelson died in 1915, their bequests were combined to make possible the construction of the museum, which is one of the finest in the country.

Born in Lawrenceburg, Kentucky, about 1835, Mary McAfee taught school before her marriage to James Burris Atkins in 1878. Although the two had known each other for years in Lawrenceburg and were thought to have been in love, Atkins honored a deathbed promise to his first wife and remained a widower for many years. Mary McAfee was in her forties when they finally married and settled in Kansas City. Atkins was an early settler of Kansas City and formed a partnership with Andrew T. Jenkins in a real estate business.

Sadly, after about five years of marriage, Mary McAfee Atkins was left a widow. Taking charge of her husband's affairs, she oversaw the burgeoning of her $250,000 inheritance to an estate of $1,000,000 at her death. The shrewd management of her husband's property throughout the city's business district (including the northwest corner of Twelfth and Main streets, the site of the Boley Building) plus a valuable tract of land in Clay County brought her an abundance of wealth that no one suspected she possessed.

Described in appearance as angular-looking with large, dark eyes behind her ever-present glasses, she was known for her intense likes and dislikes. These opinions mirrored those of her late husband. Of a sober and somber countenance, it is said that she refused to smile for a year after his death. Even though she could have bought nearly anything she desired, frugality had been a necessary fact of life in her younger years, and she saw no reason to change. Atkins refused to keep a carriage, preferring to ride the streetcar. She was not a fan of either music or literature, beyond a few travel books, and she had no interest in community affairs.

But, Atkins' annual summer journeys to Europe during the last nine years of her life seem to have fueled her passion for beauty and art. She was always alone when she traveled to places such as the National Gallery in London, the Pitti Palace, and the Louvre. She particularly favored the latter and most enjoyed the city of Geneva, Switzerland. Small objects of art found their way home to the Washington Hotel where she lived.

Mary McAfee Atkins

*Mary McAfee Atkins*

COURTESY OF THE NELSON-ATKINS MUSEUM OF ART, KANSAS CITY, MISSOURI died on October 13, 1911, while vacationing in Colorado Springs. Her funeral service was presided over by Dr. Burris Atkins Jenkins, namesake and friend of her late husband. She was buried beside her husband in Elmwood Cemetery.

Her late-blooming love of beauty resulted in the largest gift to Kansas City from a woman: $300,000 for the creation of an art museum. Twenty years later when the actual construction began, the bequest had grown substantially under the astute management of executors A.W. Childs and Herbert V. Jones.

# DOROTHY BARDEN

SHE WAS A GENUINE paradox: a life insurance salesman who at the same time was a student taking flying lessons during the early days of aviation. At the annual county fair in her hometown of Bridgeport, Nebraska, Dorothy Barden made a decision that changed the course of her life.

She was a daredevil in every sense of the word. One autumn day in 1929 she gambled her life by making her first parachute jump to earn money for flying lessons (one wonders who carried her life insurance). In those days such an activity was most unusual; Barden was aware of only a few women jumpers. But, she needed the money, so she goaded the board of the county fair into paying her $50 to jump. Her next step was to locate a parachute. One was ordered from Denver. What arrived was designed for balloon ascensions with directions for conversion to airplane usage! She followed the instructions carefully.

"Of course, I really didn't realize the awful chance I was taking. I knew enough to be scared, so scared that if it hadn't been my hometown and the announcement made and everything, I would have backed out," Barden said later.

The appointed day came. Barden left the ground in an old Eagle Rock biplane piloted by a local man with fewer than ten hours' flying experience. Gripping the fuselage so hard she was sure she would leave dents, she finally climbed out on the lower wing . . . and jumped. The parachute opened immediately, and she floated down, landing in a shallow lake.

Her career probably would have ended with that splash had a flying circus not heard of her folly. They offered her a very attractive proposition: a summer job with two jumps per week, paying the princely sum of $100 a jump. She agreed. But Barden was not lacking in good sense. Knowing from experience that her life depended upon the care with which her parachute was packed and maintained, she decided to do it herself. She learned the trade and became the first woman parachute rigger licensed by the Civil Aeronautics Board.

Dorothy Barden turned her interest in parachute jumping into a profitable business. She jumped for other circuses and amassed a total of 408 jumps by 1942, believed to be a record for women. Additionally she developed a career of teaching men and women how to jump from airplanes. But it was her third career, parachute rigging, that brought her to Kansas City.

She had operated a parachute rigging service for commercial pilots at the Oakland Municipal Airport. But when World War II began, the market dried up, and Barden decided to relocate.

William A. Ong, president of Ong Aircraft Corporation and longtime friend, was instrumental in her choice of Kansas City. The aviation industry was rapidly growing, and parachutes were an essential element of flying. Ong had a large building constructed for Barden's business, complete with a 16-foot drying loft that parachutes could be hung in and inspected. Federal

COURTESY MISSOURI VALLEY SPECIAL COLLECTIONS, KANSAS CITY PUBLIC LIBRARY, KANSAS CITY, MISSOURI

*Dorothy Barden*

regulations required bimonthly inspections, especially for damp-
ness, which slowed opening, and wrinkles, which caused tears.

During the war much of Barden's business was for the military,
rigging parachutes and supervising drop tests from airplanes using a
dummy she called Oscar. Government supervision was strict. Barden explained, "The scarcity of silk and the possibility of sabotage
makes proper inspection of parachutes particularly important at this
time as one vicious trick is to inject a slow-burning acid into the
parachute pack by means of a hypodermic needle."

Dorothy Barden gambled her life for $50 and won a new career
as one of the first women to make a successful entry into the aviation industry.

# SARAH RICKARD BARRET

T HE MULTITUDE OF things that "almost happened" are usually
insignificant. But such
was not the case for Sarah
Rickard, who claimed she
"almost" married Abraham
Lincoln.

Her story, as told in *The
Kansas City Star* in 1907,
began in Springfield, Illinois, when nine-year-old
Sarah Rickard came to live
with Mr. and Mrs. William
Butler, her brother-in-law
and sister. Butler was a
close friend of Lincoln, who
ate his meals with the family. It was there that he met
Sarah Rickard who thought
him quite nice but homely.

When she was 16 years
old, Lincoln frequently took

*Sarah Rickard Barret*

Sarah Rickard to parties and other social engagements and, she felt, hinted at marriage several times. She was sure she could have married him had she so chosen. "My name is Sarah, and one evening while Abe and I were alone together in the parlor, he became very serious and said to me: 'Now Sarah, you know your Bible well enough to know that Sarah was Abraham's wife.' I knew what was coming, so I got up and left the room. If I'd known that he would have been president, I would have paid more attention to him."

However, Lincoln began courting Mary Todd. Rickard remembered that before his marriage to Todd, Mrs. Butler, her sister, commented to him that Mary was a nice girl. Lincoln was said to have replied, "There are plenty of nice girls, and there's one I'd much rather marry than Mary. I'd rather have Sarah for my wife than any girl I know."

But Lincoln did marry Todd, and Sarah became the wife of Richard F. Barret, a longtime friend of Lincoln.

Settling in Kansas City in a cottage at 2011 Indiana Avenue, Sarah Rickard Barret must have had moments of wondering what might have been.

# LUCY STOWE BIGELOW

THE GEORGE H. NETTLETON HOME (originally the George H. Nettleton Home for Aged Women) celebrated its 100th birthday anniversary of women taking care of women in 1990. For over 50 of those years Lucy Stowe Bigelow's enthusiasm, dedication, caring, and leadership helped make possible the security and quality of life for hundreds of women.

Born in Baltimore, Bigelow came to Kansas City in 1885. Quality Hill, the most fashionable area of the city, was where she chose to live.

First and foremost she was a teacher. "I believe the greatest joy other than being a mother is that of being a teacher." In 1909 she opened Miss Bigelow's School at 729 Troost Avenue for boys and girls. An academic taskmistress, she stressed values and morals that would be practiced by her students throughout their lives. Since most of her pupils were from wealthy families who expected their progeny to continue their education, Miss Bigelow's evolved into a tutorial school with the goal of preparing students for college.

Bigelow was a woman imbued with a sharp and curious mind, and she sought other women having mutual intellectual interests. As a member of the Club of '93, she participated in discussions of numerous topics, such as the Alexandrian Period and the Greek language.

Her acquaintance with Mrs. George H. Nettleton, also a resident of Quality Hill, resulted in finding her life's dedication. Widowed in 1896, Nettleton generously donated her home at 626 Pennsylvania Avenue in 1900 for use as a permanent residence for elderly women. Bigelow, who had an interest in and sympathy for the plight of homeless women, became involved with the home shortly after the turn of the century. By 1917 when the home had moved to newly constructed quarters at 5125 Swope Parkway, she had become a member of the home's board of directors. During Bigelow's tenure, the home was enlarged with an addition of a west wing and a sun porch.

One of her best known projects was sponsoring the Nettleton Home Patriotic Circle. Formed in 1923 and composed exclusively of residents, money raised by selling their handmade products was used in aiding needy World War I veterans and their families. The women also did volunteer work at the local veterans' hospital.

Bigelow died on January 9, 1951, at 3729 Baltimore Avenue, her home of many years. She is remembered not only for teaching and her leadership at the Nettleton Home, including serving as the president of the board of directors from 1939-47, but also for other activities with the Shut-in Society, Daughters of the American Revolution, and the

COURTESY THE GEORGE H. NETTLETON HOME

*Lucy Stowe Bigelow*

Westminster Congregational Church.

When complimented on her work, she shrugged it off with, "That's what we're here for!"

# EDNA SCOTTEN BILLINGS

WHAT DO "MAMA MUSIC" and "Episcopal Mother in Israel" have in common? Both names were affectionately bestowed upon Edna Scotten Billings, an organist who played for over 50 years at Grace and Holy Trinity Episcopal Cathedral and 20 years at Temple B'nai Jehudah.

She was born December 4, 1900, in Paducah, Kentucky, the daughter of Mack D. and Cora Snodgrass Scotten. In 1902 her father, a freight conductor with the Frisco Railroad, was transferred to Kansas City. The family moved into a home on Observation Park Hill at 1205 West Twentieth Street.

Edna Scotten attended Switzer Elementary School and Westport High School. As a young girl on her way to Sunday school at the First Baptist Church, she would walk by Grace Episcopal Church at 415 West Thirteenth Street and pause to enjoy the sound of the beautiful organ music accompanying a choir of boys. She imagined playing the organ there when she grew up. When she was just 18 years old, she commuted on

*Edna Scotten Billings*

COURTESY JONED SLOVER

the old Strang Electric Line to play the organ for First Presbyterian Church in Olathe.

While at Kansas City Junior College, Edna Scotten studied organ under Clarence Sears, who for many years was the organist at St. Paul's Episcopal Church. In 1935 she received a bachelor's degree in music from the Kansas City Conservatory of Music. She also studied at the Juilliard School of Music in New York City.

Her dream to become Grace Episcopal's organist was fulfilled in 1922, and she spent 50 years with the church (now Grace and Holy Trinity Episcopal Cathedral). A hard worker with a deep inner drive, she took time from her organ duties to marry Dr. John H. Billings, a dentist, on October 19, 1927. Near the end of her career she commented that, "I've been off briefly to have two babies, my tonsils removed, and my appendix taken out. Otherwise, I've been blessed never to have missed a Sunday because of sickness."

When Mabelle Glenn resigned as the choir director of Grace and Holy Trinity Cathedral in 1945, Billings took on that responsibility. To improve the choir's diction, she studied with Fred Waring. She remained as choir director for 15 years.

*Edna Scotten Billings as she appeared in her cathedral choir robe and cap.*

COURTESY JONED SLOVER

Edna Billings was an instructor in organ at Mount St. Scholastica College, Central Missouri State University, Pittsburg State University, and the Kansas City Conservatory. Somehow she also found time to give private lessons. Among her pupils were Bettye Miller, the jazz pianist, and several local cantors.

Teaching, playing, and learning were the main elements in her life. On becoming organist for Temple B'nai Jehudah in 1951, she studied Jewish music and later studied Hebrew in order to direct the choir.

By the time of her retirement in October 1972, Billings had played before three generations of church members at the cathedral, more than 5,200 worship services, countless weddings, funerals, holiday services, recitals, concerts, and the consecration of four Episcopal bishops. In fact, it is said she wore out the big pipe organ at the cathedral.

Edna Scotten Billings was regarded by her peers as a musician of exceptional technique with an enormous repertoire. She served as the first dean of the Kansas City Chapter of the American Guild of Organists. Her last public appearance was in 1972 at the organ of Jerusalem's Anglican Cathedral. She died on March 28, 1983, and was eulogized as a woman who could never be forgotten because she gave her gifts away.

# ANNIE RIDENBAUGH BIRD

ONE OF KANSAS CITY'S mercantile giants, the venerable Emery, Bird, Thayer Dry Goods Company, had a woman as its president for 17 years. Her name was Annie Ridenbaugh Bird, and she broke new ground for women in the Kansas City business community.

Annie Ridenbaugh, the daughter of Mr. and Mrs. William Ridenbaugh, was born on April 24, 1856, in St. Joseph, Missouri, where her father was the editor and publisher of the *St. Joseph Gazette*. She remained a

*Annie Ridenbaugh Bird*

COURTESY MISSOURI VALLEY SPECIAL COLLECTIONS, KANSAS CITY PUBLIC LIBRARY, KANSAS CITY, MISSOURI

part of that city's social scene until her June 16, 1880 marriage to Joseph Taylor Bird, at which time the 24-year-old bride and her groom made a home in Kansas City.

Her husband had come from New Jersey where he had been employed in a small dry goods store. Joining the firm of Bullene, Moores & Emery in Kansas City, Joseph Bird had moved up the ladder until he was named president of the company.

From 1897 until 1904 the Birds lived at 706 West Tenth Street on Quality Hill. In 1904 they moved to the John Perry mansion at 3600 Broadway, which they named Elmhurst since it was heavily forested with large elm trees. The stone house was demolished shortly after Annie Bird's death.

Two years after her husband's death while vacationing in Colorado Springs in 1918, Annie Ridenbaugh Bird was elected president of the Emery, Bird, Thayer Dry Goods Company. It was a rare happening in the business world; in fact, it was believed that no other woman had assumed a position of such responsibility in Kansas City.

Bird accepted her new duties more as a trustee than a manager. Likening herself to a floorwalker, she had neither an office nor a desk. She preferred a role of high visibility, moving frequently throughout the store.

Charitable and philanthropic affairs grew in importance in her life. Bird contributed to the nation's war effort by financing a large World War I field hospital in France. She also remembered Kansas City, particularly Mercy Hospital, in her giving. In 1924 Bird and her daughter, Josephine Bird (later Mrs. Porter T. Hall), presented to Mercy Hospital in memory of Joseph T. Bird a deed to property in the 1500 block of McGee Street. The building on the site was sold with the proceeds enabling the dedication of the Joseph T. Bird Nurses' Home and School of Child Nursing on June 10, 1927. Bird was also a member of the Colonial Dames of America.

Annie Ridenbaugh Bird died at Elmhurst on January 28, 1937. She was buried in the family plot at Mount Washington Cemetery. Among the women of the community she was unique as not only the president of the city's largest retail establishment but also as a prominent philanthropist.

# ETHEL INGALLS BLAIR

W HO TRANSFORMED THE WEEDY, untended grounds of the Grace and Holy Trinity Church at Thirteenth Street and Broadway into a garden of inexplicable beauty? A woman by the name of Ethel Ingalls Blair who modestly attributed this remarkable change to luck and the hard work of the church janitor.

Ethel Ingalls was born in 1868 in Atchison, Kansas, the daughter of John James Ingalls and Anna Louisa Ingalls. Her father, a lawyer, poet, and statesman, was elected to the United States Senate as a Republican in 1874. Ethel, her mother, sister, and three brothers joined the senator in Washington, D.C. where she spent her girlhood. It was following her graduation from the Convent of the Visitation that Ethel made her debut on New Year's Day in 1888.

The family returned to Atchison for Ethel's marriage on October 24, 1894, to Dr. Edward G. Blair, a Kansas Citian who was a pioneer in plastic surgery.

Ethel Blair's love of nature led her to accept a request made by Mrs. Carlo Gino Venanzi, sister of Mary Rockwell Hook, who was visiting her parents in Kansas City. She asked Blair to look after the lawn of Grace and Holy Trinity Church and its few plantings.

COURTESY GRACE AND HOLY TRINITY CATHEDRAL

*Garden of Memory at Grace and Holy Trinity Church*

Though a somewhat experienced gardener, Blair launched into the project with a blissful ignorance of certain conditions in the church yard such as the soil and the location of sun and shade. The results at the end of the first summer were disheartening. A careful assessment of the situation by Blair and Jim, the church janitor, revealed that the sun-loving plants were tucked into shady corners while the shade-loving ones were baking in the blistering summer sun. Only the petunias survived, but that was enough of a victory to inspire the Garden of Memory, a memorial for loved ones and a monument to lessons learned in the church yard.

It began simply. Several parishioners expressed a wish to give a plant or have seeds sown in memory of someone. Ethel Blair also sent letters to members of the church requesting donations of less than $1.50 for the Garden of Memory. The response was overwhelming. Gradually, under her guiding hand the location took on the appearance of an English garden where flowers bloomed in place of tombstones. She planned, planted, and weeded.

There was a bed of pansies in remembrance of a child, a rose bush planted in memory of a beloved mother, and a clump of mallow and lilac bushes given by two widows for their husbands who had been childhood friends.

Crocuses planted in the shape of a cross heralded spring and late-blooming asters greeted winter. Peonies and iris were a gift of Mrs. Homer Reed, daughter of Sarah and Kersey Coates, honoring the bridesmaids at her wedding. Each year Clara Kellogg sent a donation in memory of Katherine Baxter.

Robert Nelson Spencer, rector of the church, called the garden the greatest sermon ever given there.

Ethel Ingalls Blair died December 26, 1958, at the age of 90. Burial was in Mount Vernon Cemetery in Atchison.

# JULIA B. BRADEN

THE TIME WAS 1931: America was deep in the throes of the Depression. But one local business was grossing over $1,200 a month. Surprisingly its product was popcorn and the owner and operator was a woman.

The business began when Julia B. Braden was widowed and needed a constant source of income to support her family. Given the economic conditions of the day, she realized that attaining this goal would be difficult, but she had come to know what hard work meant. Raised on a 600-acre farm in Illinois under the supervision of her German immigrant father, she had washed dishes, churned butter, and gathered eggs when she was five years old. At the age of 19 she earned money by going to other homes to sew. After her marriage she traveled with her husband selling homemade medicines, lotions, and ink door-to-door.

Following her husband's death, Braden searched for a business she both liked and could be profitable. "I wanted something steady to do. I saw popcorn stands, how clean they were, and it seemed to me that anyone used to doing the kind of work I was could run one."

She began with a stand in the lobby of the Linwood Theater at Fortieth Street and Troost Avenue in 1914. It grossed less than $15 per week for several years. To help supplement the popcorn business, Braden sold her own home-roasted peanuts. Since the theater was open only in the evenings, her workday ran from 6 P.M. until midnight when she returned home to 3042 Prospect Avenue on the streetcar. Shelling, blanching, and roasting peanuts were done early in the morning. Her regular work schedule was sixteen hours a day, seven days a week.

COURTESY MISSOURI VALLEY SPECIAL COLLECTIONS, KANSAS CITY PUBLIC LIBRARY, KANSAS CITY, MISSOURI

*Julia B. Braden*

Braden eventually made a decision to concentrate on the pop-corn trade, and business flourished. She kept her stands in the Lin-wood, Isis, Lindbergh, and South Troost movie theaters stocked with peanuts, homemade candy, and popcorn. Braden had to secure a guaranteed supply of field-grown popcorn to support her busi-ness. In 1930 she contracted for 500 acres which produced approxi-mately 1,000 pounds per acre. She also required over 100 pounds of butter a week. "Good butter it is, too. I know from my churning days good butter from bad."

She was an entrepreneur who never asked for credit, paid her bills weekly, and raised a son by herself. Depression or no Depres-sion what Julia B. Braden accomplished in the business world was extraordinary.

# MADALYNE PINKSTON BROCK

*Madalyne Pinkston Brock*

COURTESY MADALYNE BROCK WATKINS

SHE WAS KANSAS CITY'S ver-sion of the Statue of Liber-ty, for over 100,000 people became American citizens when she was the executive director of the Naturalization Council.

Madalyne Pinkston was born on November 12, 1894, in Oregon, Missouri, the daughter of Ira and Lelia Ellen Pinkston. After her father's death, the family moved to Kansas City where she at-tended a local elementary school and graduated from Westport High School. While at West Kentucky College in Mayfield, Kentucky, she mar-ried Maynor Brock who later served as headmaster of both Pembroke and Country Day schools in Kansas City.

Madalyne Pinkston Brock reared four children before participating in civic activities as a member of the Woman's City Club. In 1936 she was appointed chairman of the club's Naturalization Committee, which functioned as a local supplement to the Works Progress Administration (WPA). When the program was eliminated, Brock sought out backers. She appealed to the Community Chest, and it came to the rescue.

Brock became executive director of the Naturalization Council of Kansas City in 1938. She attended summer courses at Harvard University, Columbia University, and the New York School of Social Work during her first few years on the job to sharpen her skills.

Gentle and soft-spoken, Madalyne Brock carefully guided newcomers into the American way of life. The Naturalization Council sent a personal letter of welcome to each immigrant in his native language. The council sought to help them overcome language and cultural barriers. As executive director she didn't aid just a few people: there were about 5,000 war brides who came to Kansas City after World War II, and Brock visited each of them. Her agency aided people in dealing with immigration and naturalization papers.

She recalled a frightened young European couple who needed help. He had worked as a slave laborer in Germany during World War II and had come to Kansas City in 1951 with his wife. They credited her understanding and compassion in giving them a sense of security which enabled them to buy a home and become naturalized citizens.

Education of immigrants was a primary focus. Brock and her husband wrote *Teaching English to the Foreign Born* in 1952. The manual was used in schools and libraries nationwide. In 1962 she was instrumental in introducing a television program, "Operation Alphabet."

Madalyne Pinkston Brock received an International Merit Award from the People-to-People Council and was named Woman of the Year in 1960 by the Missouri Federation of Women's Clubs. Theta Sigma Phi, the national organization for women in journalism, presented her the Matrix Award in 1962 for her work with the Naturalization Council, and the Women's Chamber of Commerce established the Madalyne Brock Foundation that assisted in the work of the council. The fund is still active.

Brock, who retired from the Naturalization Council at the age of 80, died on March 30, 1990, at the age of 95 years.

# ESTHER SWIRK BROWN

B EAUTY BEING IN THE eye of the beholder, Esther Swirk Brown dazzled her many friends with a physical and a spiritual beauty.

Born September 17, 1917, in Kansas City, she attended Frances Willard Elementary School and Paseo High School. She studied at the University of Chicago and Northwestern University. Her major was sociology which provided the base for her career as a civil rights crusader.

After she married Paul Brown, the boy who lived across the street, in 1943, she became a typical suburban housewife living in Johnson County, Kansas. But she was much more than that.

COURTESY MARY MERRICK REEFER

*Esther Swirk Brown*

When working for the passage of a school bond issue for the South Park district of Merriam, she discovered appalling conditions in a school for black children. Their building had inadequate heating and lighting, outdoor toilet facilities, and an unqualified teaching staff. An irate Esther Brown removed the children from the school, arranged a temporary location in homes of black families, and taught classes herself. She stated, "I wouldn't want my children to go to a school like that. Why should someone else?"

When she had raised enough money to provide qualified teachers, Brown rolled up her sleeves to right what she regarded as the terrible wrong that had enabled this situation. This time she worked through the courts and won. In 1949 the Kansas Supreme Court outlawed the system of gerrymandering that deprived black children of equal education facilities and opportunities in *Webb v. Kansas*. Esther Brown also prodded the National Association for the Advancement of Colored People (NAACP) to pursue the historic *Brown v. Board of Education of Topeka* case in which the Supreme Court ruled that segregated schools deprive minorities of equal educational opportunities. (The Brown in the case was a black man.)

Civil rights and human relations, prejudice and discrimination were topics that greatly interested Esther Brown. At a meeting of the Sisterhood of Temple B'nai Jehudah she was asked to present a program on human relations. She did far more than that by helping found the Panel of American Women in 1957. Its objective was to promote brotherhood.

Sixty-three panels, made up of a Catholic, Jewish, black, and white Protestant or ethnic representative, involved 1,400 women in the United States and Canada in presenting public programs on prejudice. The approach was low-key and nonconfrontational with speakers telling of their personal experiences with prejudice. Brown became the national coordinator, assisting in the formation of dozens of panels. In 1967 she was honored for her work in the field of human rights by Theta Sigma Phi. The Brotherhood Award of the Kansas City chapter of the National Conference of Christians and Jews was presented to her in 1969.

Brown was a member of the American Jewish Committee, Jewish Community Relations Bureau, and Jackson County Civil Rights Commission. She was a founding member of the American Jewish Congress and a board member of the Missouri Association of Social Welfare.

Esther Swirk Brown, who spent her adult life promoting brotherhood, died on May 24, 1970 and was buried in Rose Hill Cemetery.

# GEORGIA H. BROWN

THE KANSAS CITY WORLD in 1903 stated that "She stands alone as the one person in Kansas City who is competent to produce any kind of entertainment the public demands." This skill was finely honed during many years appearing on stage and teaching dramatics.

Georgia H. Brown was born into a stage family. Her father was an actor, her mother an actress, and her grandfather an actor. Given this background, there was little chance she could break with tradition . . . but she had no desire to do so.

Born in Quebec, Canada, she was named Georgianne Valentin. At the age of three years she moved with her parents to Cleveland, Ohio, where she made her childhood stage debut as Little Eva in *Uncle Tom's Cabin*. When she entered vaudeville, she picked up dancing skills. Following her father's death, she teamed with her mother and traveled as the Morrell Sisters. They moved to Lawrence, Kansas, when her mother married Edward Brown. It was at this point in her life that she took the name of Georgia Brown. She married Charles Vaughan and had a daughter before her husband's death. Her second marriage was to Maurice Quincey.

*Georgia H. Brown*

COURTESY MISS SUSANNAH GENTRY

In 1900 Brown came to Kansas City and soon began teaching and staging ballets and dances for the Priests of Pallas. Named after Pallas Athena, patron goddess of Athens, the event included a parade and ball and eventually grew into Kansas City's most elaborate civic and social function. Brown directed the ballet performed by several hundred girls in 1912.

However, it was as a drama coach that she excelled. Serving first as the director of the Woodward School of Acting, she later opened the Georgia Brown Dramatic School. When she was joined by her daughter Evelyn, the studio was on the first floor of a building located at 911 Grand Avenue. They later moved to 3212 Troost Avenue.

Brown frequently expressed her love of youngsters. She tried to give each and every aspiring five-year-old her undivided attention. Since several of her students went on to work on the stage, her fame was national. Jeanne Eagels studied with her and after becoming a star sent Brown a bowl of roses with a note reading, "To my first and only teacher—to whom I owe everything."

Georgia H. Brown died on October 31, 1932, and is remembered as a woman with a youthful outlook on life who never grew old or forgot how to laugh.

ENTRANCE

The Georgia Brown Dramatic School

THE LITTLE THEATRE

3212 TROOST AVENUE

*The Georgia Brown Dramatic School Entrance,
Souvenir Program, Class 1915-16*

COURTESY MISS SUSANNAH GENTRY

# SARA SMITH BUSCH

IT WAS JUST like a fairy tale: a beautiful young girl born in Fayette, Missouri, met a handsome young Danish musician, and it was love at first sight . . . and they married and lived happily ever after.

Sara "Sally" Smith was the last of ten children born to a country doctor and his wife, Thomas Jefferson Smith and Margaret McCullough Holmes Smith. The large, musical family enjoyed a home life with the traditional hospitality and refinement of the Old South. By the age of six years the baby of the family was practicing daily on the family's square piano.

After two years at Howard College, at the age of 15 she came to Kansas City to study music. While attending a concert, she met a young Danish violinist named Carl Busch. They fell head over heels in love and married six days later in her family home. It may have been impulsive, but it proved to be enduring.

Since both of them wanted a career in music, the newlyweds went abroad to study. She worked under Bruno Zwintscher and Carl Reinecke, the conductor of the Vienna Orchestra, at the Leipzig Conservatory. Sara Busch won the Helbigschen Prize, one of the highest awards at Leipzig, for playing the Grieg Piano Concerto in A minor. She then studied with Teresa Carreno in Austria.

*Sara Smith Busch*

During this time, her young husband continued his study of violin and composition.

By 1896 Sara Busch was recognized as one of the world's most accomplished pianists, displaying an elegant technique in her many performances. But, she found that her life as a concert pianist required too much time away from her husband. She transferred her enthusiasm to teaching and became a leading instructor recognized not only in Kansas City but also in the United States. The Busches moved into the Studio Building where they lived and taught.

Sarah Busch also had other interests. She was a member of the Kansas City Musical Club and was involved in the founding of the Woman's City Club.

Carl Busch was knighted by the King of Denmark in 1912 and by the King of Norway in 1922. But, in Kansas City success was more elusive. The Kansas City Philharmonic, which he started in 1895, disbanded after several years due to a lack of public interest. His wife, absolutely firm in her belief in her husband's talent, was greatly disappointed. During the Depression their livelihoods were greatly impacted by the economic times, and her health began to fail.

Sara Smith Busch died on March 25, 1939. She was a magnificent musician and teacher and a woman utterly devoted to her beloved Danish violinist for 50 years.

*Sara Smith Busch*

# ANNIE CHAMBERS
## Leanna Loveall Chambers Kearns

$S$HE WAS MATRONLY, white-haired, with a firm chin and conserva-
tive dress—but for many years ran a "resort," an infamous
establishment in Kansas City's red-light district.

Leanna Loveall Chambers was born near Lexington, Kentucky,
on June 6, 1843. As a pretty teenager, she was invited to ride in a
parade supporting Abraham Lincoln's presidential bid. Her father,
who was adamantly against the Yankee, claimed she had disgraced
the family so she
moved to an uncle's
home. She began
teaching school
and married Wil-
liam Chambers.
Their first child
died in infancy.
During her second
pregnancy Leanna
Chambers was
thrown from her
buggy while out
for a ride. As she
lay in a coma, her
husband died from
a fall and her sec-
ond child was
born dead.

*Annie Chambers*

After this twin
tragedy she decid-
ed to go to Indi-
anapolis and have
a "short life but a
fast and merry
one." Merry yes,

short no. She became known as Annie Chambers, a prostitute, and lived to be 92 years old. Falling in love with a handsome client, she was sure marriage was again in her future, but those hopes were dashed when she met his wife and children in 1869. Deeply disappointed, she packed her bags and came to Kansas City.

Annie Chambers opened her first house of prostitution, known as a resort, on the north side of the Missouri River. Realizing the city was moving southward, she built a 25-room mansion at 201 West Third Street in the heart of the city's red-light district in either 1871 or 1872. She had rules for some rooms of the house. "I wouldn't allow the girls to smoke in the parlor; it would have given the place a bad name." To the west of her house was one run by Eva Prince, and one block away was Madame Lovejoy's. Chambers married and divorced William Kearns.

A madam with a heart of gold and a mother hen to her girls, she helped girls with no place to go, and when they wanted to leave, helped them get a new start. Appearing before the city's all-male Society for the Prevention of Commercialized Vice Committee in 1913, she said: "When they [the girls] come to us they have no place to go. . . . It was always the same story . . . it was their employer, his son, or someone with whom they worked who was responsible for their downfall. If there only was more chivalry among men, there would be far less vice."

The city ordered her mansion door closed in 1921, but a determined Annie Chambers got it reopened in 1923 and then closed it herself so that she could operate a legitimate boarding house, principally for railroad men.

When Reverend David B. Bulkley established the City Union Mission in the heart of the red-light district, he and his family moved into the house next door to Annie Chambers. He preached a funeral sermon, the first she had heard in over 75 years, that moved her deeply. "But, it wasn't the first time I had wept in 75 years. People think women of my sort are hardhearted, but we have hearts, too. . . . I had two babies of my own that died." In 1934 with Bulkley's encouragement, Chambers was saved from a life of sin and in gratitude bequeathed her home to the City Union Mission.

Annie Chambers died on March 24, 1935, in her vermilion bedroom on her made-to-order brass bed.

# BERENICE MENARD CHOUTEAU

THERE CAN BE LITTLE doubt that She qualifies as Kansas City's original pioneer mother for Berenice Menard Chouteau was the first
white woman to make her home in this area. She was born in 1801
in Kaskaskia, Illinois, the old French capital on the Mississippi River.
Her father, Colonel Pierre Menard, the first territorial governor of
Illinois, made sure his daughter was carefully reared and properly
educated.

However, at the age of 18, her life completely changed when she
became the bride of François Gesseau Chouteau. The 24-year-old
groom was the nephew of Auguste Chouteau, a co-founder of St.
Louis, and had just become a partner in the American Fur Company.

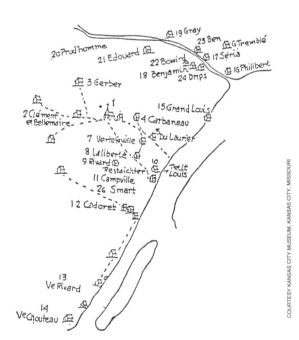

François and
Berenice Chouteau
made a two-month
honeymoon trip up
the Missouri River
from St. Louis in a
keelboat accompa-
nied by 30 French
voyageurs and trap-
pers traveling in a
flotilla of canoes.
They went as far as
St. Joseph before
returning. In 1821
they made another
trip and landed at a
location that has
come to be known
as Randolph Bluffs
on the north side of
the Missouri River
in Kansas City.
There in 1821 Fran-
çois Chouteau began

COURTESY KANSAS CITY MUSEUM, KANSAS CITY, MISSOURI

*Map from* Wilderness Kingdom, Indian Life in the
Mountains: 1840-1847. *The Journals and Paintings of
Nicholas Point, S.J., translated and introduced by Joseph P.
Donnelly, S.J. (Loyola University Press). Berenice Chouteau's
residence is "14 Ve Chouteau" (widow Chouteau).*

building a trading center that served men sent by the American Fur Company to trap the Missouri, Kaw, Platte, Osage, Arkansas, and Neosho rivers. It remained in this location until the flood of 1826.

Initially, Indians posed a threat, but gradually the Chouteaus developed a friendly relationship with them. Berenice Chouteau learned nursing skills so she was able to treat the French and the Indians when a cholera epidemic broke out which claimed the lives of two of her four children. In gratitude for her services, a number of Indians converted to Christianity.

The Chouteaus, who were ardent Catholics, constructed a small chapel and altar in their home. In 1833 Father Benedict Roux came to the area, and the Chouteaus supported his work with time, work, and money. Berenice sewed his vestments.

François Chouteau had acquired considerable acreage in an area along the south bank of the Missouri River near what is now Independence and Prospect avenues, and in 1838 he patented an adjoining 160 acres. Shortly afterward, he died.

With a big family and growing business responsibilities, Berenice Chouteau decided to build a large house. Construction began about 1850 at Third Street and Troost Avenue; the home was not finished three years later when she sold it and over 500 acres of land to Joseph Guinotte. He completed the house for his Belgian bride Aimee, who became a close friend of Berenice Chouteau.

The Chouteau family moved to a large, white colonial house at Pearl and Market streets, an area that later became the first Quality Hill. Among the furnishings was a piano, the second in Kansas City (John C. McCoy owned the first).

Tall, erect, and dark-haired, Berenice Chouteau was regarded as a woman with considerable vigor. Her exact appearance is unknown because she refused to sit for a portrait or have a photograph taken.

In 1886 she filed a lawsuit challenging the title to much of the West Bottoms, the land she and her husband had first settled. She lost the suit two weeks before her death. Judge John Philips ruled that she had "slept upon her rights" too long.

On November 19, 1888, Berenice Menard Chouteau died at the home of a daughter-in-law, Mrs. M.A. Chouteau, at 1410 East Ninth

Street. She had outlived nine sons and one daughter. Sixty-nine years after her honeymoon trip up the Missouri River she was laid to rest beside her husband in St. Louis.

# SARAH CHANDLER COATES

IN 1859, JUST TWO YEARS before Fort Sumter was shelled, Sarah Chandler Coates took up permanent residence in Kansas City, a town with a population of less than 5,000 and a southern boundary at Twentieth Street. Actually, she had come to live in the Town of Kansas because the name Kansas City did not become official until 1889.

It was a frontier town for the many travelers who passed through on their way west on the Santa Fe, Oregon, and California trails. The lack of refinement must have been, if not a shock, at least trying to Coates since she came from a family of culture.

She was born on March 10, 1829, in Kennett Square, Chester County, Pennsylvania, the daughter of John and Maria Jane Chandler. Her father was a Quaker and had served as a state senator from 1824 through 1827.

Sarah Chandler graduated from a Philadelphia seminary, taught school,

*Sarah Chandler Coates*

COURTESY MISSOURI VALLEY SPECIAL COLLECTIONS, KANSAS CITY PUBLIC LIBRARY, KANSAS CITY, MISSOURI

and married Kersey Coates, a lawyer whom she had met in Philadelphia. The following year she came with him to Kansas City.

It was during her temporary stay in 1856 and 1857 that the Eastern bride had a disquieting experience precipitated by the border ruffianism of "Bleeding Kansas." While living in the Gillis House, a hotel located right on the Missouri River levee between Delaware and Wyandotte streets, Coates hid Andrew H. Reeder. He was the first Territorial Governor of Kansas and was fleeing from bands opposing his stand against slavery. For two weeks she helped conceal him before his escape to Chicago. Coates returned to her childhood home for a year before coming back to Kansas City in 1859.

She and Kersey Coates moved into a two-story brick house located on the southwest corner of Tenth Street and Pennsylvania Avenue. They owned 120 acres of land that is now Quality Hill. Colonel Coates (he earned the rank in the Civil War) was well on his way to becoming one of the city's greatest community leaders.

Sarah Coates was intelligent and sought ways of fulfilling herself. Through her efforts the History Club, later called the '82 Club, was organized. The clubs' objectives were to provide an opportunity for women to increase their knowledge and participation in humanitarian causes and to expand their knowledge of history, literature, science, and art. She was one of the founders of the All Souls Unitarian Church and an officer of the Kansas City Athenaeum.

A steadfast clubwoman as well as a woman of mettle, Sarah Coates was said to have been closely identified with almost every charitable effort in the city. She served as an officer of the Woman's Christian Association, the first charitable organization in Kansas City, and was a member of the Visiting Nurse Association, Helping Hand, Kansas City Women's Exchange, Protestant Home Association, and Mother's Club. A resolute supporter of women's suffrage, she was president of the local Equal Suffrage Association.

Sarah Chandler Coates died on July 25, 1897, and was buried beside her husband in the family plot in Elmwood Cemetery. She was a doer and faithful supporter of community causes.

# CAROLYN BENTON COCKEFAIR

SHE WAS A YOUNG 63 years old when she joined the faculty of the University of Kansas City as an assistant professor of English and was still young when she retired at the age of 80.

Carolyn Belle Benton was born on November 30, 1884, in Greenton Valley near Odessa, Missouri. She was a descendant of one of the first families of Virginia and was the fifth daughter of Richard Higgins and Alice Johnson Benton. Her parents, who were farmers, instilled a love of learning in their children. "I cannot remember the time when I could not read or when I had no interest in books," Carolyn Cockefair said of her youth.

She attended elementary school and her first two years of high school in Odessa. But, her parents wanted more cultural activities available to their daughter so they moved to 1005 Harrison Street in Kansas City. She graduated from Central High School and entered the University of Missouri at Columbia. By 1908 she had completed a bachelor of science degree in education, a bachelor of arts in English, and a master's degree in English. In the process she earned a Phi Beta Kappa key. She taught in a Centralia elementary school for $30 a month and then in Columbia for $45 a month.

Her first fulltime post was as the assistant principal in the University of Missouri's demonstration school in Columbia. She began to develop her own style of teaching: the Socratic method in which the leader asks questions

*Carolyn Benton Cockefair*

but gives no answers. Her enthusiasm and rapport with her students made it work.

She met and married William Raymond Cockefair, a successful farmer, in 1911. They moved to Black Water Farm which he managed, and for the next 12 years she took care of two daughters and one son.

Beginning in 1922, Carolyn Cockefair substitute taught in the English Department at Central Missouri State Teachers College. In 1925 she accepted a position in the extension division of the University of Missouri. Since the curriculum was heavily oriented toward agriculture and home economics, Cockefair added the humanities—literature, poetry, music, and philosophy. Reading the classics became a requirement for her courses. Cockefair became a master of leading her students in discussions from which she seldom chose to withhold her strong opinions.

In 1941 Carolyn Cockefair accepted an assistant professorship at Central Missouri State Teachers College. Dr. Norman Royall, dean at the University of Kansas City (now University of Missouri-Kansas City), knew of her success in the classroom and invited her to join the faculty in 1947. Assistant Professor Cockefair met and captivated her students, including many World War II veterans and women eager to return to school, with her unorthodox teaching methods.

She was not impressed with the state of education in the country. "Education is America's biggest business. Yet America, the greatest business nation in the world, tolerates mediocrity in the schools that it would never tolerate in business." There were higher standards in her classroom.

With Dr. Royall she began a local Great Books program that proved to be so successful that the original four discussion groups grew to be forty. A university division was created that evolved into the department of continuing education. Adult education was one of her primary goals.

But, Cockefair was not highly regarded by all her university colleagues. She held no doctorate and had not published a scholarly work so she taught only introductory freshman and continuing education classes. When asked about this situation some years later, she responded, "I became accustomed to dealing with people for whom innovation and popular acclaim constituted a threat."

Her students gave her high marks and joined friends and Mrs. Selma Feld in establishing the Carolyn Benton Cockefair Chair in Continuing Education.

Cockefair retired as a professor emeritus in 1964 and died on December 1, 1969. Thorpe Menn, literary editor of *The Kansas City Star*, wrote that "Her total viewpoint was outward from herself. . . . She was a woman devoted to learning and teaching."

# MARY ELIZABETH COLTER

*Mary Elizabeth Colter*

COURTESY MARY COLTER: BUILDER UPON THE RED EARTH, BY VIRGINIA L. GRATTAN

SHE WAS A 33-year-old art teacher from St. Paul, Minnesota, with no formal training in architecture when she went to work for the Fred Harvey Company. Mary Colter later became its chief architect, designer, and decorator.

Born on April 4, 1869, she was the daughter of William and Rebecca Crozier Colter who ran a clothing store in Pittsburgh, Pennsylvania. The family moved several times before settling in St. Paul.

There was a large Sioux population in that area, and Colter owned and adored a few of their drawings. When a smallpox epidemic swept through town, she hid the artwork from her mother who was burning all Indian items in the house in hopes of preventing further spread of the disease. The drawings remained with her throughout her life and were a source of inspiration.

With little encouragement from her parents, she postponed pursuing her art interest until after her father's death when she enrolled in the California School of Design. Tuition was $2.50 per month. Art courses were her first choice, and to help supplement a meager budget Colter sought employment in a local architectural firm as an apprentice. Her income was still not adequate so she returned to St. Paul to begin a 15-year teaching career at Mechanics High School. In 1902 she went to work for the Fred Harvey Company. Later she came to Kansas City where she lived for over 25 years, much of that time at the Rockhill Manor.

The Harvey Company operated hotels, restaurants, gift shops, and newsstands in the Atchison, Topeka, and Santa Fe Railroad stations. Harvey and the Santa Fe Railroad employed Colter to design the interiors of several stations. Her first job was the Indian Building in Albuquerque (demolished in 1970).

In 1905 she served as both architect and decorator for the Hopi House, designed of wood and stone to resemble a Hopi pueblo. Constructed on the rim of the Grand Canyon, the building broke away from traditional European styles that were in vogue. Colter believed that a structure should be in harmony with the environment as well as a visual reflection of the local culture. These ideas were unsettling to Harvey executives, but Colter prevailed. Her work can still be seen in this, her architectural triumph, as well as the Watchtower, Bright Angel Lodge, and other buildings along the rim of the canyon.

Colter worked in her office in Kansas City Union Station to design La Posada, the railroad station at Winslow, Arizona, and plan the remodeling of the La Fonda Hotel in Santa Fe. The original decorator of the Harvey Company Gift Shop and eating facility in Kansas City's station, she later remodeled the dining facilities and added a cocktail lounge, the Westport Room. Colter designed the furniture made of bleached aspen and Swedish birch and commissioned Hildreth Meiere to paint a mural depicting the early days of Westport.

She retired from Santa Fe Railroad Company in 1944 after 29

years of service. In 1948 she left Fred Harvey Company after 46 years. Mary Elizabeth Colter died at the age of 88 leaving an impressive architectural legacy.

# LOULA LONG COMBS

THE QUIET IN THE American Royal arena was almost deafening. Soon a whisper grew into an explosion as the gates were thrown open, and the queen of the American Royal made her entrance driving a hackney. She sat straight as an arrow and was elegantly attired, wearing a $350 Parisian hat adorned with three birds of paradise. (Recalling that her father had scolded her for paying $35 for another hat, she said, "I will bill each bird separately so it won't be such a shock.") Loula Long Combs was doing what she did best.

*Loula Long Combs*

Born on January 30, 1881, in Columbus, Kansas, she was the daughter of Robert A. and Ella Long. The family moved to 2514 Independence Boulevard in Kansas City where her father continued in the lumber business with partner Victor Bell. Long-Bell Lumber Company became the world's greatest privately held lumber company.

Loula Long adored horses and made her show debut in 1896 at Fairmount Park in Kansas City where she won the five-gaited class. She continued riding and winning locally at first and later nationally and internationally.

In 1911 the Long family moved to Corinthian Hall, a 72-room mansion at 3218 Gladstone Boulevard. It was designed by Henry F. Hoit, who also did the buildings at Longview Farm. There were over 40 buildings on this magnificent country estate where Loula Long's horses were stabled.

All her harness horses' names ended in *ion* to signify her stable. One animal was extraordinary. In her eyes, no horse could rival Revelation, who came to her as a three-year-old in 1909 and became the greatest heavy harness horse in his time. His breeding was undistinguished: his sire was The Tramp, a racing trotter, and his dam a farm mare with no particular lineage. From his first showing in Denver until his last in the same town in 1924, Revelation won more than 60 blue ribbons and trophies. When he died at Longview Farm in 1935, she had him buried near the show barn. "I resolved I would never love another horse as much."

Loula Long, a most eligible heiress, had suitors by the score, reportedly including a Polish prince, a grand duke, and a famous American horseman. But she found her own prince charming. One day she saw a team of horses struggling to pull a heavy coal wagon up a hill. The driver was beating the horses, and she rushed over to stop him. A man intervened, attached the wagon tongue to the axle of his car, and pulled the wagon to the top of the hill. That night at dinner she told her family, "If he isn't already married, I'm going to marry that man." She did. In 1917 Loula Long became the wife of Robert Pryor Combs, a man who encouraged his wife to continue her career in the show ring.

Loula Long Combs won acclaim throughout the United States and Canada. She was one of only two people from the horse show world chosen for the Hall of Fame at Madison Square Garden.

Her 60-year career was brought to a close at the American Royal in 1961. In her George IV phaeton, pulled by prize hackneys, she was dressed in a wide-brimmed hat and a long dress. Loula Long Combs received a ten-minute standing ovation from the appreciative crowd.

Baseball fascinated her. If not in the Long-Bell box watching home games, she was sure to be listening to the radio.

Longview Farm was a frequent site of balls and horse shows

with proceeds going to charity (frequently animal shelters). A 146-acre tract of its land was donated as the campus for Longview Community College.

Loula Long Combs died on July 5, 1971. She was interred with her husband at Forest Hill Cemetery.

# ELIZABETH BRUCE CROGMAN

SHE LIVED A SELFLESS life of concerned dedication to pregnant girls and unwed mothers in the black community.

Elizabeth Bruce was born on May 1, 1894, in Pittsburgh, Pennsylvania. As the bride of prominent physician W.H. Bruce she came to Kansas City in the early 1920s and immediately became involved in community affairs. An Urban League volunteer, she regularly visited the Juvenile Court of Jackson County where she developed a deep interest in the girls she saw. "I used to go to juvenile court, and I would feel sorry for these girls because they didn't have any place to go, and they didn't have any place to leave their babies because their parents didn't want them and they couldn't go to the white Crittenton home, so I felt that I had to do something." She knew what she wanted to do; the question was how to do it.

A fortuitous encounter with William Volker, the well-known Kansas City philanthropist, provided the

*Elizabeth Bruce Crogman*

COURTESY MRS. EARL THOMAS AND MRS. CHARLES B. WILKINSON

answer to her dilemma. He promised to pay for a home for the girls if she would find an appropriate structure. In September 1925 Bruce opened the Florence Home at 2446 Michigan Avenue, a four-bedroom dwelling that was a place to live for unwed mothers and their children. Serving as mother to all who lived there, her goal was the moral, mental, and physical rehabilitation of the women.

It rapidly became evident that the home was too small. Bruce again contacted Volker for assistance. This time he agreed to donate $10,000 toward the purchase of a larger building if the community would match the gift. Bruce became a one-woman fund-raiser. Mrs. William Marty responded to her call by donating a lot at Twenty-fourth and Campbell streets. Bruce's dedication and unflagging energy enabled funds to be raised, and in 1930 a new four-story building opened with facilities to care for 30 women and their babies. Physicians and nurses from the community volunteered their time in the hospital and nursery. Counseling and classes in cooking, sewing, general housekeeping, crafts, and Bible study were offered. Bruce served for about 20 years as the home's director before retiring in 1945.

Following her divorce from Dr. Bruce, she married Dr. Leon C. Crogman, a dentist from Lorraine, Ohio, who was the brother of Ada Crogman Franklin, the wife of the founder of *The Call*. After her husband died, she returned to Kansas City and lived in a house at 4645 Benton Boulevard.

Continuing to do community work until 1991, Elizabeth Bruce Crogman died on January 23, 1992. She was buried in St. Mary's Cemetery. Many of her 97 years of life were spent as a strong advocate of women.

# MINNIE LEE CROSTHWAITE

SHE WAS ONE OF Kansas City's first black social workers and a highly respected community leader.

Minnie Lee Harris was born in Nashville, Tennessee, on February 28, 1872, one of the two children of James and Harriette Anne Harris. After attending public schools, she enrolled in Fisk University preparing for a career in teaching. For two years she taught first grade in a Nashville public school before resigning in 1889 to marry David N. Crosthwaite, the principal of the first all-black Nashville high school. They moved to Kansas City in 1895 when Dr. Crosthwaite joined the faculty of Lincoln High School. Her husband had a medical degree but preferred teaching.

When Crosthwaite's three children were old enough that they did not require her full attention, she opened a hairdressing parlor at Ninth and Central streets and later a flower shop, which she sold in 1918. It was not retailing but social work that became her life's focus.

She began her real career in 1920 as a volunteer with the Provident Hospital Association. She liked to recall that she was one of only four social workers in the area at that time. Minnie Crosth-

*Minnie Lee Crosthwaite*

waite decided to take a nine-week course in social work at the New York School of Social Welfare to hone her skills. In 1922 she became a full-time social worker at Wheatley-Provident Hospital and later was named director of the hospital's outpatient clinic. She remained in this position until her retirement in 1947. During her tenure she was active in the founding of the Mercy ward for children at the hospital, working closely with Dr. Katherine B. Richardson.

Crosthwaite served for 21 years as president of the hospital's Auxiliary No. 1 and coordinator of an annual fashion show and evening of entertainment for the benefit of Wheatley-Provident. Big bands under the direction of such famous names as Cab Calloway, Duke Ellington, and George Lee attracted huge crowds. Held first at the Labor Temple at Seventeenth and Vine streets, the shows were later moved to the Municipal Auditorium. During the 20 years of her leadership money was raised to help pay off the hospital's mortgage, buy an X-ray machine, modernize the kitchen, and purchase and remodel a home for nurses.

Not all of her time and energy went to the hospital for Crosthwaite participated in several community endeavors. She was one of the first members of the Women's League, a group that backed the introduction of manual training into Kansas City public schools; organized the local order of the Daughters of Isis; served as president of both the local and state chapters of the National Association of Colored Women; and was a member of the American Association of Social Workers, Booklovers Club, YWCA, and NAACP.

Minnie Crosthwaite died on January 9, 1963, at the age of 90. The funeral service was held at the Second Baptist Church where she had been a member for more than 68 years, and burial was in Highland Cemetery.

# MILDRED DeVILBISS

YOU'RE PLUMB CRAZY to leave a position like this for the uncertainty of a business of your own." So spoke P.W. Henry, president of South Side Bank. It fell on deaf ears for Mildred DeVilbiss had made up her mind to leave a steady paycheck and a successful banking career so that she could sell rugs.

While still an employee of the bank, she had made rugs by hand as a hobby in a home at 316 East Sixty-ninth Street where she lived with her sister and widowed mother. DeVilbiss purchased Colonial Rug Studio, 1020 East Seventy-fifth Street, in 1944.

In her new business DeVilbiss offered four types of rugs for sale: braided, hooked, crocheted, and woven. Braided rugs were the most popular. Customers for the handmade products lived far and wide— from the Pacific Coast to New England, from Texas to Michigan, and all around the Midwest.

The shop's mail order business made up a large portion of the profitable operation. Her "hooker" business supplied wool cuttings for people who hooked rugs.

Mildred DeVilbiss succeeded as a woman in a man's world of commerce.

*Mildred DeVilbiss braiding a rug at her Colonial Rug Studio.*

# MARY SCHERRILL DICKERSON

S HE REFERRED TO IT as indulging in a costly whim, and indulge she did, initially to the tune of $7,000 for a horseless carriage. That was a princely sum for the early 1900s, and with it Mary Scherrill Dickerson became the owner of the most expensive automobile in Kansas City. This was but the beginning of a spending spree that ended with a veritable stable of cars.

Born in Geneva, New York, she and Dr. D'Estaing Dickerson were married in 1863, the same year her father was killed in the Battle of Gettysburg. Two years later they moved to Kansas City where her husband opened a general practice of medicine that was closed at his death on May 3, 1902. Dr. Dickerson left an estate of over $1 million.

Mary Dickerson remained in the family home at 1120 Wyandotte Street until 1905 when she purchased a large stone mansion on the northwest corner of Armour Boulevard and Main Street for

*Mary Scherrill Dickerson's $7,000 beauty which she drove in the early 1900s.*

$50,000. The house had been built by Robert L. Taylor, a brother of John Taylor who opened the John Taylor Dry Goods Company.

More than financially secure, Dickerson began satisfying her passion for horseless carriages. If not an eccentric, she was regarded with much curiosity for at that time women were neither owners nor drivers of automobiles. She enjoyed the thrill of speeding, and many a horse-drawn carriage was startled as she raced by at 30 miles per hour. Mounted police knew her well, and at least once she was caught and fined $250 for speeding. Her eccentricities included refusing to allow men to ride in her cars. When she lent a car to a female friend, it was on the condition that no men were allowed to be in it.

Her collection of cars included a French model, several Pierce-Arrow limousines (these were her favorites and cost about $8,500 each), and her town car.

Dickerson died at her home on July 26, 1909 and was buried in Elmwood Cemetery. Several months following her death her automobiles were auctioned off on the steps of the federal building as the funeral of Colonel Thomas H. Swope passed by. One of the purchasers was B. Haywood Hagerman, the father of Carol Durand.

# CAROLYN DOUGHTY

C AN YOU IMAGINE," she said, "I probably have the widest acquaintanceship in the city and possibly the most friends—their children, nieces, sisters, aunts, and grandmothers." It's not surprising because Carolyn Doughty served as the executive secretary of the Woman's City Club for nearly 50 years.

Born in Clinton, Missouri, Carolyn married William J. Doughty, and the couple made Kansas City their home. He died not long afterward. In 1918 the Woman's City Club hired her as a waitress but soon realized her capabilities. Because she had all the necessary skills to work with club members, her position was changed to hostess. In less than a year she was working fulltime. "I don't know just when or how I stopped being hostess and became executive secretary. Like Topsy, my job just grew."

Organized in 1917 by Mrs. James C. Coburn and 30 other

women interested in education, music, art, philanthropy, and civic affairs, the members of the Woman's City Club met at 408 East Eleventh Street. A few years later the club moved to 1111 Grand Avenue. The management of the club was Doughty's responsibility. She even served ex officio on all committees and assumed the job of club historian, keeping a history in scrapbooks.

Under Doughty's watchful eye, excellent food, quiet reading rooms, distinguished speakers, and an atmosphere of good fellowship became hallmarks of the Woman's City Club. She worked long and hard to achieve this. Doughty combined great executive ability, exceptional charm (especially with men), and an abundance of tact and resourcefulness. She was always prepared for the unexpected. For example, opera star Madame Ernestine Schumann-Heink was brought to Kansas City to speak to a luncheon meeting of the Woman's City Club. Unfortunately, her trunk of clothing was lost en route, and she refused to keep the engagement in her travel clothes. Leaving orders to keep the members eating, Doughty rushed to the hotel and explained to the singer that 350 members were eating their desserts and eagerly awaiting her appearance. With that, the diva smoothed her clothing, put on a hat, and fulfilled her obligation.

Doughty and the Woman's City Club initiated the outpatient clinic at General Hospital, instituted the mothers' milk station that provided milk for premature and sick babies, ran 12 public playgrounds, and provided funds for the care of children whose mothers were giving birth in the hospital. One of Doughty's favorite events was the annual Christmas carol luncheon held at the Woman's City Club with songs by the boy's choir of the

*Carolyn Doughty*

Grace and Holy Trinity Episcopal Cathedral under the direction of Mabelle Glenn with piano accompaniment by Edna Scotten Billings.

In 1943 the Woman's City Club started the Carolyn Doughty Trust Fund for Children. The money has been used to equip the Rehabilitation Institute, the speech and hearing departments of the University of Kansas Medical Center and the General Hospital, Spofford Home, Gillis Home, Children's Mercy Hospital, and Minute Circle Friendly House. When $20,000 was donated for playground equipment for Guinotte Manor in 1992, a total of more than $350,000 had been disbursed by the fund to help disabled, disadvantaged, and needy children.

Carolyn Doughty died on January 21, 1975, in La Jolla, California, where she had made her home after retirement in 1964. When asked one time how she viewed her job with the Woman's City Club, she replied, "Job? It's not a job. Why the club is my hobby."

# LUCY CHRISTIE DRAGE

*Lucy Christie Drage*

S HE HAD GOOD TASTE, a love of nature, and artistic talent, which were the bases for the profitable business she founded. Lucy Christie Drage was a leading interior decorator of her day.

She was born on September 18, 1876, the daughter of C.C. Christie, a Kansas City grain broker. She grew up on Quality Hill near her dearest friend, Julie Woollcott, sister of Alexander Woollcott, American journalist, wit, and taleteller. After attending Miss Barstow's School on Quality Hill, she enrolled in Kansas City Art Institute. She was a dark-haired beauty and

much a part of the social activities of the city. In 1900 she was chosen belle of the Century Ball held at the old Convention Hall.

Romance entered her life when Captain Francis B. Drage, who
had received his commission in the British Army during the Boer
War, came to Kansas City with a party of fellow officers. The dash-
ing young captain, a member of the Royal Horse Guards, met and
married Lucy at the Christie home in one of the major social events
of the season.

After living in England for ten years, the Drage family returned
to the United States. Lucy Drage became business manager of the
Christie farm located just south of town. Colonel Drage died in
1935 at the Drage estate in England.

Widowed with three grown children, Lucy Drage decided to
start her own business. Since she loved flowers, gardening, and
houses, she decided to merge her interests and decorate the interior
of homes. Her goal to bring the outdoors inside was accomplished
by making chintz, the quintessential English floral fabric, her decorating signature.

Lucy Drage Interior Decorating, Inc., opened at 320 Ward Parkway with Ethel Guy, her associate for many years. Her philosophy
of decoration was summed up as "Good taste, with warmth and
color . . . after all, a fireplace and dogs about and flowers—chintz

Ethel Guy                                                      Lucy Drage

## LUCY DRAGE, Inc.
(The CHINTZ SHOP)
320 Ward Parkway, The Country Club Plaza
Va. 4579
Kansas City, Missouri

flowers!—are a good start toward furnishing a home."

She received many important commissions from prominent
Kansas Citians. Sorority houses at the University of Missouri in
Columbia and the University of Kansas benefited from her talents
as did the newly completed Kansas City Club at 1228 Baltimore

Avenue. While the Kansas City Country Club was under construction, Drage, a club member, worked with architects and the decorating committee on the furnishings.

Tragedy touched her life but did not stop her. On April 20, 1936, her daughter and son-in-law, Elizabeth and Frederick H. Harvey, vice-president of Fred Harvey Systems, were killed when their Beechcraft biplane crashed.

Drage was a successful businesswoman, active member of many organizations, and, later in life, a talented amateur painter. She was the local chairman and co-founder of the national Bundles-for-Britain campaign during World War II and a founding member of the Fireside Group of the Kansas City Art Institute. In 1962 she was elected a fellow of the American Institute of Interior Decorators.

Lucy Christie Drage died on September 11, 1965, and was buried in Forest Hill Cemetery.

# CAROL HAGERMAN DURAND

DURING A RELATIVELY short lifetime she earned a place on the United States equestrian team but was denied the honor of competing in the 1952 Olympic games because she *was* a woman.

Carol Hagerman, the daughter of B. Haywood and Helen Eaton Hagerman, was born in Kansas City on August 4, 1918. Her first interest in riding came early; when she was just seven years old she won a trophy in competition at the American Royal. Only a year later she began riding jumpers.

She attended Sunset Hill School, Baldwin School in Bryn Mawr, and Smith College. Before graduating from Smith, Hagerman joined the American Red Cross during World War II, serving 22 months, seven of which were spent in the China-Burma-India theater of war. While in Burma, she drove a 12-wheeler army truck in a Red Cross canteen convoy along a 200-mile stretch of road from Namkan, Burma to Paoshan, China. She also found time to join a jungle hunt in which a 300-pound tiger was killed. Shortly after the war, she married Frederick Dana Durand, an insurance agent in

Kansas City. They were parents of one son.

Following the war, Durand began to make a name for herself in local and national equestrian competitions that she won with regularity. In 1950 in an international competition held in Toronto she became eligible to compete for a place on the United States equestrian team that would participate in the 1952 Olympic games. But there was one enormous hurdle: women had never been admitted to the Olympic jumping contests. But, Durand was hopeful and began an intensive training regimen.

Her skill and determination were rewarded when she was chosen to be one of the three members of the U.S. Olympic team that would compete in the Prize of Nations category in Helsinki. She was the first American woman accorded the honor. But within two months, the Federation Equestrian Internationale barred Durand from competition because "Women have never competed in the games against men." Despite this disappointment Durand remained on the Olympic team for four years. She must have derived some satisfaction in winning an international stake at the National Horse Show in Madison Square Garden on November 8, 1953. She rode Reno Kirk, the horse she would have ridden in Helsinki.

Durand was associated with the equestrian program at Stephens College for over 25 years and was listed in *Who's*

COURTESY MARY ELLEN PURUCKER

*Carol Hagerman Durand*

*Who of American Women, 1958-59.* Her life ended on September 28, 1970, when evaluating a jumper that reared and fell on her. She was buried at Mount Washington Cemetery.

Carol Hagerman Durand is remembered for the joy she found in teaching children to ride and for her fearless spirit and great love of the sport. In 1983 she was inducted into the Greater Kansas City Amateur Sports Hall of Fame.

# JEANNE EAGELS

*Jeanne Eagels*

SHE WAS BORN with a passion for make-believe and an inner resolution to become famous. But hers was a Cinderella story without a happy ending because Jeanne Eagels, Kansas City's most famous stage actress, died when she was just 35 years old.

Amelia Jean Eagles was born in Boston on June 26, 1894 (there is some question about the year), the second child of Edward and Julia Eagles. The family moved to Kansas City two years later. At the age of five she began studying drama with Georgia H.

Brown, whom she credited for her success. Jean Eagles began participating in local pageants, festivals, and church plays. When not yet a teenager she made her stage debut as Puck in *A Midsummer Night's Dream*.

A few years later, she worked as a bundle inspector at Emery, Bird, Thayer Dry Goods Company, while trying to break into show business. Dubinsky Brothers Tent Repertoire Company hired her, and for the next several years she toured with it, playing in tents and living in one hotel room after another. It was rumored that Morris Dubinsky was the true love of her life. During this time she changed the spelling of her name to *Jeanne Eagels* because she thought it would read better up in lights.

With extensive theatrical experience and a striking beauty, she went to New York in 1911 where she labored in minor parts and movies for ten years. Eagels' greatest achievement came when she starred as Sadie Thompson in John Colton and Clemence Randolph's play entitled *Rain*, an adaptation of Somerset Maugham's "Miss Thompson." Fame and fortune were hers. The play opened on November 7, 1922, and ran for over 650 performances, of which Eagels missed only seven. But a problem with alcohol became serious. Broadway producer David Belasco remembered her telling him that "Pain makes me drink. I hate to drink; I know it will be my undoing and people won't understand, but I have to drink. I can't help it." During this time she married Edward H. Coy, a former Yale University football player turned New York City banker. They were divorced three years later.

After *Rain* she took the leading role in a French farce, *Her Cardboard Lover*. After 100 performances on Broadway, the production went on tour. Eagels failed to appear at a performance in St. Louis claiming ptomaine poisoning, but the Actors' Equity Association insisted the absence was related to her drinking. She was fined and suspended by the association for one year.

She worked in vaudeville and motion pictures during her suspension. Her film debut was in *The Letters*, a 1929 Paramount sound release. During filming there were a number of temperamental outbursts, believed to have been fueled by alcohol, but her performance was noteworthy and earned her an Academy Award nomination for best actress.

On October 3, 1929, while she was being treated for a "nervous" condition, Jeanne Eagels collapsed, convulsed, and died. Death, according to a New York City toxicologist, was due to an overdose of chloral hydrate, a sleeping medication. Her body was returned to Kansas City aboard the Twentieth Century Limited. After a funeral service at St. Vincent's Catholic Church, she was buried in Calvary Cemetery.

Edward Doherty in an article that appeared in *Liberty* Magazine wrote that Jeanne Eagels "was a genius and drunkard—artist and hellion—poet and devil."

# MARY ELIZABETH EPPERSON

U.S. EPPERSON DIED IN 1927, leaving to his widow not only a fortune but also his special affinity for the arts in Kansas City. In a loving gesture, Mary Elizabeth Weaver Epperson devoted the

*Mary Elizabeth Epperson*

remainder of her life to promoting art and music as a memorial to her husband.

Born on a farm near Cooperstown, New York, she moved with her parents, Mr. and Mrs. William Weaver, to Kansas City where she attended St. Teresa's Academy. Her first meeting with Epperson kindled a romance that soon blossomed into marriage. Her husband was president of the U.S. Epperson Land & Development Company and the U.S. Epperson Underwriting Company. For recreation he helped organize the Epperson Megaphone Minstrels while longing for the time to be an artist. Their marriage was childless.

After she was widowed, Epperson became a true patroness of the arts. She was one of the largest contributors to the Kansas City Philharmonic, endowing the general fund and the music library. In 1927 she began planning a major gift to the Kansas City Art Institute. The new U.S. Epperson Hall had a $90,000 auditorium and exhibit gallery with a small stage suitable for intimate musical programs and art lectures. She also paid for the construction of an impressive gateway leading from the art institute to the Nelson-Atkins Museum of Art. Additionally, Epperson purchased a residence at 4446 Oak Street for $50,000 and presented it to the art institute for use as studios and classrooms.

Shortly before Christmas in 1938, Epperson donated to the Municipal Auditorium over 100 old theater bills and photographs that her husband had collected. That same year she contributed $2,000 to the Conservatory of Music for instruments and music.

Epperson's generosity was a marvelous tribute to the memory of her husband. But there was one memorial to her: the scores of elm trees she had planted on the grounds of their home at 5200 Cherry Street. She made sure they received daily watering during Kansas City's scorching summers. The home was willed to the University of Kansas City (for many years the Epperson House was home of the university's school of education).

In March 1938 Karl Krueger and 40 Philharmonic musicians performed a concert at her home out of appreciation and admiration for her support. Mary Elizabeth Weaver Epperson died on October 22, 1939, at the age of 84. Her funeral service was conducted at her home and attended by more than 200 of Kansas City's social and cultural leaders. For two hours the Kansas City Art Institute, University of Kansas City, Conservatory of Music, and Kansas City Philharmonic were closed in her honor.

# PHOEBE JANE ROUTT ESS

PHOEBE JANE ROUTT ESS, the dean of Missouri clubwomen, was a tireless worker for a vast number of causes. She used her organizational ability, her gift for public speaking, and her influence to ensure that things got done.

She and her twin sister began life on March 3, 1850, on a farm near Versailles, Kentucky. In 1854 their parents, Kenneth and Olivia Downs Routt, decided to join the westward movement and journeyed with their rosewood furniture, paintings, and silver to Liberty, Missouri (they thought it had more promise than Kansas City). The twins enrolled in the Clay County Seminary.

The family moved to Kansas City in 1872, and Phoebe Routt became a teacher in the upper grades at Washington School. A

*Phoebe Jane Routt Ess*

COURTESY JACKSON COUNTY HISTORICAL SOCIETY ARCHIVES

woman in those days was expected to choose between marriage and a career. She chose both. She enjoyed her job and continued it until her marriage in 1875 to Henry Newton Ess, a partner in the highly respected law firm of Karnes & Ess. After her marriage she chose a new career.

The roles of wife and mother of one son and two daughters kept Phoebe Routt Ess fully occupied for several years. In 1882 she joined the Tuesday Morning Study Club. Because of her membership in this organization, she participated in the founding of the General Federation of Women's Clubs in 1889.

During more than 50 years working for civic causes, Phoebe Ess compiled a monumental list of accomplishments. A staunch supporter of women's suffrage, she was one of the founders of the Susan B. Anthony Civic Club in 1913, serving as president for 23 years. Despite strong opposition she traveled the state carrying the banner for a woman's right to vote, and owing largely to her efforts, Jackson County was one of the first Missouri counties to adopt women's suffrage. She also fought for Prohibition.

For the sake of children Ess lobbied the Kansas City Public School District for playgrounds and art in the classrooms. To preserve justice and fairness for all, she was involved in establishing the Jackson County Parental Home for Girls as well as serving as a strong advocate of legal protection of widows and children.

Horrified by stories she heard about the treatment of prisoners in Missouri's penal system, she campaigned for an investigation which resulted in an improvement in prison conditions.

In the fall of 1893, Mrs. Laura Everingham Scammon invited several women, including Ess, to meet and discuss Plato. They planned to form a women's club "for the purpose of promoting mutual sympathy, and united effort for intellectual development, the improvement of social conditions, and the higher civilization of humanity." A constitution, drafted by Dr. Martha Dibble, was signed by 58 women, among them Phoebe Ess, Mary Harmon Weeks, Mrs. Hugh McElroy, and Florence Logan. The club was named the Kansas City Athenaeum, and Ess served as its treasurer.

Her friends and associates claimed that Ess had a role in the foundation of over 30 clubs and movements. Her club affiliations included the League of Women Voters, Jefferson Democratic Club, Woman's City Club, Mother's Day Nursery, Mothers and Children Society (out of which grew the Parent-Teacher Association), and the Welfare League for the Prevention of Crime and Delinquency. She also served as a director of Lincoln and Lee University and the Missouri Federation of Women's Clubs (1923-26). After World War I, she circulated petitions advocating world peace and disarmament, which were presented to the League of Nations in Geneva, Switzerland.

In 1918 she allowed her name to be placed in nomination on the Citizens ticket for the Kansas City Missouri School Board. Although not elected, she was the first woman in Kansas City to run for public office.

She never stopped working for others. During the Depression, shortly before her death, she told her son that during the previous six months she had knocked on doors and placed 63 needy people in jobs.

Phoebe Routt Ess died on April 10, 1934, at the home at 1300 East Thirty-second Terrace she shared with her twin sister Betty P. Turner. She was buried in Elmwood Cemetery.

# MARY TIERA FARROW

FOR OVER 50 YEARS she was hailed as the dean of women lawyers in Kansas City. But early in her career when she applied for membership in the all-male Kansas City Bar Association, one of the members declared, "No sir-ree. We don't want any petticoats as members or attending our meetings." And so she was blackballed by the bar.

Mary Tiera Farrow was born May 27, 1880, in Columbus, Indiana, the daughter of Alva Curtis and Martha Haiselup Farrow. When she was five years old, the family moved to Delphos, Kansas, where her father opened a general store. She grew up listening to stories told around the store's potbellied stove about Abraham Lincoln's virtues and local court trials. She was enchanted.

After finishing high school in Garnett, Kansas, Tiera Farrow came to Kansas City where she enrolled in a business school. With her certificate in hand, she found her first employment as a "typewriter" with a Kansas City, Kansas grain firm. The dress code for women was strict and uncomfortable: two or more starched petticoats, a shirtwaist dress, and a high stiff collar. While men were allowed to doff suit coats, roll up sleeves, and loosen ties and stiff collars during steamy summer days, there were no allowances made for women employees. Office work, Tiera Farrow decided, was not for her.

She chose to pursue a law degree and entered the Kansas City School of Law in 1901. The class had over 80 men and no other women. At first her classmates ignored her, but they soon discovered her quick wit and intelligence, and she was accepted by the group.

"I'm a lawyer, a real lawyer!" she exclaimed when she was handed her diploma. The piece of paper was fine, but employment was essential. After several rejections she was hired for $60 a month by Dail & Carter, a law firm on the Kansas side of the state line.

She worked hard and made a name for herself. In 1907 she

FROM *LAWYERS IN PETTICOATS* BY TIERA FARROW

*Mary Tiera Farrow in her Kansas City School of Law graduation dress.*

was elected the City Treasurer of Kansas City, Kansas, the first woman to hold public office there, and was reelected in 1909 and 1911. Deciding that she needed a change, she traveled abroad. Upon her return Farrow opened a law office with Anna L. Donahue, a fellow Kansas City School of Law graduate, in the New York Life Building at 20 West Ninth Street. The firm handled a variety of divorces, wills, and other small cases, one of which thrust her into the spotlight.

Farrow represented Mrs. Clara Schweiger in a simple divorce case. When Mrs. Schweiger shot and mortally wounded her ex-husband, she again turned to Farrow. Local newspapers had a field day writing about a woman charged with murder who was represented by a woman lawyer. The trial began February 26, 1916, before a packed courtroom. Farrow's defense of her client was so adept that the jury returned a verdict of second-degree murder.

In November 1916 she was appointed a divorce proctor by Judge W.O. Thomas of the Jackson County Circuit Court. Her appointment was the first public recognition as a lawyer by her peers.

Her main interest was centered on women and law. In 1917, Farrow and 20 other women law school graduates agreed to form a professional group. The Women's Bar Association of Kansas City was founded on November 8, 1917, with Farrow as its first president. A few weeks later she was asked to assist in the formation of a state-wide association, and on March 27, 1918, the Women's Bar Association of Missouri became a reality.

Farrow joined the National Guard during World War I and was assigned to the motor corps. After the war she married and then divorced. She entered the University of Illinois, studied sociology and political science from 1919 to 1922, and received an A.B. After attending Columbia University on a scholarship and completing a master's degree, she

*Mary Tiera Farrow in her World War I motor corps uniform.*

COURTESY KANSAS CITY MUSEUM, KANSAS CITY, MISSOURI

returned to Kansas City and the practice of law. Farrow and Louise Byers opened a women's school of law in 1925. The first graduating class had 14 students.

Farrow retired in 1957 from the Kansas City Welfare Department where she had served for many years as a counselor and legal advisor. It brought to an end a professional record of achievement equaled by few women. She was the first woman in Kansas City to open her own law office, the first woman municipal court judge in the city, and the first woman to appear before the Supreme Court of Kansas on an appealed case. She was fluent in French and German, and her outstanding academic record included certificates from the Sorbonne and Oxford University. She even found time to write *Lawyer in Petticoats*.

In a moment of reflection she remarked, "I have been privileged to live long enough to see women lawyers, first considered as freaks and facetiously referred to as 'hen lawyers' and 'Portia perils,' become recognized despite their sex."

Mary Tiera Farrow died November 9, 1971, at the age of 93. She is buried with her family in Garnett, Kansas.

# FLORENCE M. FENNER
# ADA M. KASSIMER

THERE WEREN'T ANY men associated with Gift Shop Necessities Company, a successful business which was started by women, employed women, and sold its products to women.

It began in 1921 when Florence M. Fenner and Ada M. Kassimer with only $68 between them opened a business. What they manufactured were called *beautilities*, a word Kassimer coined to describe utilitarian products that were also items of beauty for the home.

The design and decoration of apartments and houses underwent a change in the 1920s when kitchens were incorporated into the living area. Fenner and Kassimer sensed that a new market was opening up before their eyes and decided to give everyday kitchen items a dash of color and a spritely design since the objects would be seen more.

Theirs was a complementary partnership. Kassimer, who had worked for the Kansas City Symphony Orchestra, was imaginative and eager to test new ideas. Fenner had the business sense; she knew what would sell and counted the cost before anything was produced.

They rented rooms in a building located at 3309 Troost Avenue, subletting all but one since the operation was small. But not for long. They decided to add decorated pottery to their line. Mixing bowls, candy jars, and cookie boxes became beautilities as did perfume bottles, dorines, and jardiniers. Housewives eagerly bought all the company could produce.

The clay for the pottery was brought to Kansas City from Calhoun, Missouri, and the workers, mainly girls attending the Kansas City Art Institute, modeled the pieces that were fired in kilns at Pittsburg, Kansas. Upon their return to Kansas City the items were decorated.

The first year's sales totaled $2,700, the next year's doubled, and the numbers kept growing. Several new items were added to their line, including decorated metal hose racks, novelty match safes, and

*The factory building at 2619-21 Cherry Street.*

mail boxes. Outgrowing the space on Troost Avenue, in the spring of 1928 they moved into a building they had constructed at 2619-2621 Cherry Street. In 1929 the business produced over 1 million items and employed 25 women.

Fenner and Kassimer combined the best of artistry and business sense and made a name for themselves in Kansas City. Gift Shop Necessities Company was run for over 35 years by the two women.

# ADA CROGMAN FRANKLIN

A LOVING DAUGHTER believed in and practiced her father's favorite maxim, "They live forever who live for others." She grew up to be Ada Crogman Franklin, the mother of American black journalism, and she will not be forgotten.

Ada Crogman was born in Atlanta around 1886, one of eight children of Dr. and Mrs. William H. Crogman. Her father was a distinguished scholar, professor of Latin and Greek at Clark University for 37 years, and the first black president of the university. She graduated from Clark and taught for several years at Alabama State and Tennessee State universities before entering Emerson College in Boston where she earned a degree in dramatics.

Armed with her college degrees and teaching experience, the young, dynamic black

*Ada Crogman Franklin*

COURTESY *THE CALL*

woman won a job as a dramatics specialist with the National Playground and Recreation Association of New York. She traveled the country searching for talented blacks. The knowledge she gained propelled her into writing and producing a pageant on the history and contribution of black Americans. *Milestones of a Race* was performed and acclaimed nationwide.

During a performance in Kansas City for Wheatley Hospital she met Chester Arthur Franklin, a young printer from Texas who had founded *The Call*, a Kansas City newspaper for the black community. They married in 1925, and she immediately began writing feature stories on the local black population. The Franklins were strong proponents of equal rights for blacks and supported the passage of a federal anti-lynch law. Such legislation was never passed, but the campaign did raise public awareness.

She was firmly committed to the policy of publishing a paper that reported worthwhile happenings and achievements among black people that was free of gossip and sensationalism. Additionally, Ada Franklin was active in the business end of the newspaper. When Chester Franklin died in 1955, Ada Crogman Franklin became publisher of *The Call* and Lucile Bluford editor. They maintained the high standards of the newspaper, supporting the civil rights movement of the 1960s and promoting racial understanding.

Ada Franklin devoted considerable time to community projects. She served on the board of the Niles Home for Children, was a member of the Wheatley-Provident Hospital Women's Auxiliary, and was an active supporter of the Urban League and the NAACP. In 1969 she received the Curators' Award in Journalism from Lincoln University and the Distinguished Publishers Award given by the National Association of Newspaper Publishers in 1973. Franklin was also a member of the board of trustees of the William Allen White School of Journalism at the University of Kansas. In 1982 she donated her father's extensive collection of books, prints, and photographs to Atlanta University.

Ada Crogman Franklin, who for 58 years was associated with *The Call*, died on December 24, 1983. In remembering her friend and business associate, Lucile Bluford of *The Call* commented, "Throughout her life she sought to improve the communication among people of her city, the nation, and the world."

# MARTHA ZIMMERMAN FRANKLIN

S HE WAS THE consummate businesswoman and club member who worked tirelessly for community betterment. Martha Zimmerman Franklin was dedicated to increasing the role of women in public service.

Born on April 29, 1898, in Farmington, Missouri, she was the daughter of Lonnie and Mary Zimmerman. She attended elementary and high school in Farmington where her father was with a lead mining operation.

After her marriage to W.E. Franklin she joined him in his business, Monkey Cleaners and Dyers, Inc. at 3600 Troost. She began as secretary and later became president. According to her son, the business received its name when W.E. Franklin's original partner went to California and left behind his pet monkey.

The force of Martha Franklin's community service commitment began in 1940 as president of the Women's Chamber of Commerce (she served an unprecedented four terms from 1940 to 1944). Under her leadership, the chamber became one of the most active groups in the city, working to improve Kansas City and aiding in World War II efforts. Her work was nationally recognized when she was one of the first women selected to the Committee on Domestic Distribution of the Chamber of Commerce of the United States during the war. In 1952 the U.S. Chamber of

*Martha Zimmerman Franklin*

COURTESY THE JACKSON COUNTY HISTORICAL SOCIETY ARCHIVES

Commerce appointed her to the Committee on Advertising. Two years later Franklin was named Woman of the Year by the Women's Chamber of Commerce of Kansas City.

Additionally, she served on a number of commissions and boards. In 1942 Mayor John B. Gage appointed her to the Municipal Auditorium advisory board. Franklin was the first woman to hold the position and became board chairman in 1948.

Human needs during World War II bore heavily on her. With her son serving in the U.S. Navy, Franklin did her patriotic duty as vice-president of the local Service Men's Club and a regular volunteer at the Kansas City Canteen. In 1944 she served as vice-chairman of the Committee on Russian War Relief of Greater Kansas City.

Franklin also had an interest in crime prevention and juvenile justice. Judge Ray G. Cowan of the Jackson County Juvenile Court appointed her a member of the Merit Board in 1948 to aid in the selection of juvenile court personnel. In 1955 she became the first woman to serve on the Kansas City Crime Commission.

Franklin was president of the Soroptimist International of Kansas City; vice-president of the Advertising and Sales Club; member of the Business and Professional Women's Club, Woman's City Club, Midwest Inter-American Relations committee, Citizens Association, and the Women's National Aeronautical Society; and on the boards of the Kansas City Safety Council and Kansas City Philharmonic Association. The Women's Chamber of Commerce established a scholarship at the University of Missouri-Kansas City in recognition of her 41 years as a board member.

Looking back on her lifetime of community service, she said, "Only the most dyed-in-the-wool reactionary would refuse to admit these days that women are not only more active in public affairs but that their help in solving today's problems is more necessary than ever. The job is just too big for men to tackle alone." Martha Franklin died on December 29, 1976.

# CAROLYN FARWELL FULLER

$S$HE WAS A DYNAMIC leader in politics, music, and education, yet she had grave doubts about the possibility of becoming the first woman member of the Kansas City Board of Education. Conventional wisdom held that a woman's place was in the home or behind a desk in a classroom. But, the public had no such doubts and gave Carolyn Farwell Fuller a 67,000 vote margin of victory.

Born in 1875, she came to Kansas City from New England when she was 15 years old. With a fine contralto voice, she decided to study at the Des Moines Conservatory of Music and then in Chicago so that she could pursue a concert stage career. After her marriage to Joseph Voorhees she continued a busy schedule of concert and church appearances. From 1899 to 1907 she was in the music department of Central High School. Widowed in 1909, she married George W. Fuller, vice-president of the Fidelity Savings and Trust Company and former president of the Kansas City Parks Board.

In 1921, the year after women received the right to vote, she was approached about being a candidate for

COURTESY KANSAS CITY YOUNG MATRONS

*Carolyn Farwell Fuller*

the Kansas City Board of Education, on which no woman had ever served. She accepted the opportunity, ran for the office, and won. On April 13, 1922, Fuller took the oath of office and became an advocate of practical education. Vocational training and physical fitness were of particular interest to her, but she also insisted that cultural activities for the students of Kansas City not be slighted. She served two terms from 1922 to 1934 and chose not to run for a third.

Carolyn Fuller founded organizations, served as president of several, and was a member of many more. During her third term as president of the Kansas City Athenaeum, she founded the Athenaeum Young Matrons, which supported social, educational, and charitable causes. With her advice and guidance the Athenaeum Young Matrons severed ties with the Kansas City Athenaeum and became the Kansas City Young Matrons. Fuller was named an honorary member.

She organized the Round Table of Presidents and Past Presidents in 1917 to coordinate efforts among the numerous women's clubs. This made the work of women's clubs more focused and effective. After three terms as president, she was named honorary president.

Other organizations benefited from her membership. Fuller was a charter member of the Kansas City Musical Club and served two terms as president. She was also the president of St. Joseph Hospital Auxiliary, the Kansas City Chapter of Pen Women, and Twentieth Century Club, the Republican women's political organization which she helped found. Other civic activities included membership in the Round Robin Club, Catherine Hale Home for the Blind, and Kansas City Rose Society. She organized 1,800 women who raised $125,000 for Lincoln and Lee University in less than three weeks.

Carolyn Farwell Fuller, who is remembered as a gracious and generous woman who left a lasting mark on Kansas City, died on June 19, 1944. She donated her 500-volume library to the Kansas City Young Matrons which established the Carolyn Farwell Fuller Library in their clubhouse.

# DOROTHY GALLAGHER

THERE WAS A TIME when Mexicans in Kansas City were strangers in a strange land. But, when the doors of the Guadalupe Center were opened, all that changed, and it was Dorothy Gallagher's generosity that made it happen.

She was born on January 8, 1894, in Kansas City, the daughter of John Anthony and Florence Nightingale Gallagher. Her father was president of Faxon-Gallagher Drug Company located at 720 Broadway. For many years the family lived at 5235 Rockhill Road.

After attending local parochial schools, Gallagher graduated from Trinity College in Washington, D.C., in 1915 and later received a master's degree in social work from Washington University in St. Louis. Returning home, Notre Dame de Sion asked her to teach history in its newly opened high school. She accepted.

A goodwill mission just before Christmas gave direction to her life. When her class of students distributed food and gifts to needy families in the Mexican community, Gallagher was struck by their plight, realizing the need existed 365 days a year. When school was out, she left teaching and resolved to learn and do something about the situation.

She joined the Agnes Ward Amberg Club, an organization of Catholic women that operated a small clinic serving the population around Our Lady of Guadalupe Catholic Church. These residents were hampered by their lack of knowledge of English and American

*Dorothy Gallagher*

culture. Gallagher persuaded her mother and sister to join her in buying three bungalows at Twenty-third and Jarboe streets, which were used to house classes and other activities.

Gallagher decided to build a new community center and drew up the initial plans herself. The architectural firm of Raney & Corman completed the final plans for the two-story, Spanish-style building at 1015 West Twenty-third Street that was dedicated in 1936. The total cost for the center exceeded $50,000.

The Guadalupe Center provided child and adult programs with classes in physical education, homemaking, English, and health. It contained a gymnasium, kitchen, dining room, clubroom, offices, and a library with books in English and Spanish. It was also a place for the community to gather for socializing. Each year the center would sponsor a fiesta that attracted crowds from the entire region.

Gallagher commented, "One of our early endeavors was to have Mexicans taken to General Hospital. We finally convinced the city's health department that with the help of our Spanish-speaking caseworker as interpreter, Mexicans could be treated there."

Gallagher served as the center's head resident and director for more than 18 years, living in the staff quarters on the second floor. She served without pay. Due to the program's success she literally worked herself out of the job in 1944. Shortly after her resignation, the Catholic diocese bought the center.

In 1946 she participated in the American Aid to France program. During the year she spent in France, she worked to reestablish war-damaged health and recreational centers.

After her return to the United States, Gallagher was a caseworker supervisor and field instructor in the Jackson County office of the Missouri Division of Welfare for two years. She taught students from the University of Kansas School of Social Work and joined the faculty of the College of St. Teresa in 1949. From 1953 to 1955 she was chairman of the Jackson County division of the Welfare Association.

Gallagher served as a member of the board of the Urban League and was a member of the American Association of University Women, National Association of Social Workers, Mediaeval Academy of America, and the Fellowship House. She was one of the founders of Catholic Charities. In 1957 the Missouri Association for Social Welfare presented its award for outstanding service in health and welfare to Gallagher for her efforts in founding the Guadalupe Center.

Dorothy Gallagher died on August 14, 1982, at the age of 88. She is remembered as a woman who cared enough to devote her time and considerable personal assets to a center that served the Mexican community.

# MABELLE GLENN

WE WERE LOOKING for a man," said I.I. Cammack, superintendent of Kansas City Missouri Public Schools. "Women were teachers and musicians, but had they the necessary executive ability as well?" To the surprise of many, including several distinguished males who had applied for the position of director of music, the school board decided to appoint Mabelle Glenn. Though she had not even applied for the job, her name was on each list of recommendations prepared by five universities.

Born on March 5, 1881, in Oneida, Illinois, Glenn graduated from Monmouth Conservatory of Music in 1908. She came to Kansas City in 1921 from Bloomington, Illinois, where she had

COURTESY JONED SLOVER

*Mabelle Glenn*

been the director of music in the Bloomington public schools for ten years. Her Kansas City home for many years was at 3809 Walnut Street with her sister, Ida Glenn, who taught art at the Kansas City Teachers College.

One of her most important career achievements as director of music for Kansas City public schools was in music appreciation. She radiated a love for music and an ability to teach it: Glenn made it fun to learn, to listen, understand, and enjoy music. It became an integral part of the development of both children and teachers. When asked what she considered the most important phase of her work, Glenn replied, "Organization. Every child of the 75,000 attending public schools is given a chance for self-expression at some time during every school day." A ten-cent piano lesson was introduced in the schools so that more children could afford training.

Glenn developed the novel concept of having a concert series supported by children, believed to be the only one in the country at the time. Ten thousand children each paid $1 for a season ticket to the Kansas City Philharmonic children's concerts.

Glenn led choruses of 7,000 to 8,000 students drawn together from the public schools throughout the system. She also organized annual band and orchestra, glee club, and a cappella choir festivals. She remained as director of music for 29 years before her retirement in 1950.

Shortly after her arrival in Kansas City she also assumed the directorship of the Grace and Holy Trinity Episcopal Church Memorial Boys' Choir that was endowed by Laura Nelson Kirkwood. For the 23 years Glenn led it, Edna Scotten Billings served as its organist.

Glenn was not only a teacher but also a nationally recognized leader in her profession. She was elected president of both the National Association of Music Supervisors, the first woman in many years to be so honored, and the National Music Educators. She broadcast a series of music appreciation lessons on radio. Glenn also edited *The World of Music*, a standard series of textbooks for children from kindergarten through junior high school. She was the recipient of two honorary doctorates in music and served on the faculty of the Kansas City-Horner Conservatory of Music.

Mabelle Glenn died on August 28, 1969, at the age of 86. This talented and energetic woman put the soul into the music program of Kansas City public schools for 29 years.

# CLAUDE GORTON

W E BELIEVE THE MEN have made a muddle out of things, and now it looks as if it's up to the women to get together and talk politics instead of bridge or teas or any other kinds of parties." Claude Gorton was never a woman to mince words. (Her unusual first name was a never-ending source of confusion since people assumed she was a man before they met her.)

Born in 1888 in Marion, Alabama, she came to Kansas City as a young adult, married George H. Gorton, and was widowed in 1930. Claude Gorton was introduced to reform politics through the National Youth Movement of the 1930s and as chairman of the Independent Coalition of American Women for Missouri that supported Alf Landon's presidential bid in 1936.

Known for her quick tongue, keen mind, and graciousness, Gorton became a leader in motivating women to work in politics. Her female army played a very significant role in the 1940 city election in which they worked against the Pendergast machine and wore lapel pins in the shape of a broom, symbolic of sweeping corruption out of city hall. She served as chairman of the women's division of the United Campaign, a coalition of reform groups. Gorton was the sparkplug that got women to the polls. The reformers were successful, and John B. Gage was elected mayor of Kansas City. (Also elected on the

COURTESY JACKSON COUNTY HISTORICAL SOCIETY ARCHIVES

*Claude Gorton*

reform ticket as city councilman from the second district was Russell F. Greiner, the author's grandfather.)

Politically, Gorton was an enigma to her friends. At the national level she frequently supported Republican candidates but was adamant that she be called a Democrat. She said, "Don't you call me a 'mongrel' Democrat. I have the purest of Southern Democrat blood in my veins."

In addition to her political work, Claude Gorton was vice-president of W.B. Young Supply Company. Known as "Mrs. Kansas City," she worked to get playgrounds constructed in parks and for almost 15 years served as chairman of the city's public recreation advisory board. She was one of the founders of the United Service Organization (USO) in 1941. Gorton was active in the Travelers' Aid Society, president of the YWCA, and member of the Kansas City Philharmonic Association, Woman's City Club, Kansas City Conservatory of Music, and Kansas City Art Institute.

In 1954 she moved from her home at 5400 Sunset Drive to Louisiana, Missouri, to be near her daughter, Mrs. Charles G. Buffum, Jr. Claude Gorton died on July 5, 1975, at the age of 87 and was buried in Riverview Cemetery in Louisiana. She was a brave and forthright woman who loved the city and was instrumental in getting rid of the Pendergast machine.

# LENA HAAG

IT WAS NOT UNTIL she died that her name was made public as the donor of a liberal arts building on the campus of the University of Kansas City, forerunner of the University of Missouri-Kansas City. Although the building opened in 1937, stones above the front and back doors of the building remained blank until 1951, when it was revealed the building had been given by Lena Haag in loving memory of her parents.

Lena Haag, born May 26, 1864, was one of the three children of Rosa and Joseph Haag, German immigrants who had come to America seeking freedom and opportunity. The family lived in a home near Fifteenth and Walnut streets until Lena was five years old when they moved to the southwest corner of Eleventh and Central streets. This remained her home for over 50 years. Joseph Haag was a real estate investor in Kansas City.

Educated in Kansas City schools, Lena Haag left home to attend Moravian College for Women in Bethlehem, Pennsylvania, where her interest in art and music developed and grew with her parents' encouragement. Following graduation, she returned to Kansas City and continued to study art, becoming an able amateur painter. She was also an excellent pianist.

Upon the death of her mother, who had been widowed several years earlier, Lena Haag was willed a large estate in 1919. She nurtured the funds, firm in her belief that she was a mere custodian of the inheritance. She felt she was responsible for its growth and use to memorialize her parents. To this end, Haag sought investment advice from William Volker, a close friend and philanthropist.

Ever mindful of and grateful for everything her parents had given her, Haag wanted to provide similar opportunities for others. With Volker's assistance she decided that a building on the campus of the University of Kansas City would be a fitting memorial to her parents. Haag Hall was constructed at a cost of over $250,000. This was not her only gift to the university: she set up a $100,000 student loan fund and an endowment fund estimated at between $300,000 and $400,000.

Haag was active in a number of civic organizations, including Research Hospital Women's Auxiliary, Kansas City Athenaeum, Woman's City Club, and Kansas City

*Lena Haag*

COURTESY PHOTOGRAPH COLLECTION, UNIVERSITY OF MISSOURI-KANSAS CITY

Rose Society. She was a member of the board of the Kansas City Art Institute for many years. A dedicated traveler, she visited most European countries and circled the globe twice.

Lena Haag was 87 years old when she died on July 15, 1951. She is entombed in her family mausoleum in Forest Hill Cemetery.

# CATHERINE CONDON HALE

"DON'T WORRY, EUGENE, I'll teach you to dance and to play bridge. You can have as much fun as if you could see." These were the words of encouragement spoken by Catherine Condon Hale to her despondent brother, who had lost his vision when he was in his twenties. She did what she said she would do . . . and more. He went on to become not only a dancer and a bridge player but also a lawyer.

Catherine Condon was born November 22, 1868, in Chicago to Daniel McGrath and Ann Connors Condon. She graduated in 1885 from St. Francis Academy in Columbus, Nebraska. Five years later she married James Henry Hale, who brought his wife to Kansas City where he was superintendent of the Cudahy Packing Company plant in the West Bottoms. The couple had seven children.

*Catherine Condon Hale*

COURTESY JACKSON COUNTY HISTORICAL SOCIETY ARCHIVES

Catherine Hale and her brother went to Budd Park on Labor Day in 1911 where 30 blind persons founded the Allied Blind Workers of Kansas City. Hale became very active in the group and organized the Kansas City Association for the Blind a few years later.

With $50 from the Allied Workers' treasury, she set out to start a home for blind women. Hale and a handful of women solicited donations of furniture, rented a house at 2908 Flora

Avenue for $25, and spent the remaining $25 on groceries. The home was opened in 1919 and was immediately filled. Female residents were taught handicrafts that were sold to provide income. They were so appreciative of all that had been done for them that they insisted that the home's name be changed to the Catherine Hale Home for Blind Women in her honor. Later a larger house was bought at 2918 Tracy Avenue.

Hale wanted to provide jobs for blind workers. Through the donation of six months' rent by J.J. Heim, a partner in Heim Brewery, Hale opened a workshop at 415 West Sixth Street. In it blind men produced brooms, mats, and other handmade items which had to be marketed to wary retailers who were skeptical about quality. With the assistance of a friend, Hale loaded a car with brooms and went door-to-door and store-to-store in the West Bottoms, selling everything they had. The business was launched. A new and larger workshop was built at 1844 Broadway.

She also founded the Rockhurst Circle and was a member of the Woman's City Club and Kansas City Musical Club. Hale was president emeritus of the Kansas City Association for the Blind. She played a role in establishing the women's auxiliary of St. Joseph Hospital.

Catherine Condon Hale, the good Samaritan of the blind community, died at her home at 3217 Summit Street on July 6, 1947.

# EMMA MARCUS HALL

IT WAS A MAN'S WORLD—or so it would seem—since keeping her job with a bank depended upon concealing the fact that she was a woman.

Emma Marcus Hall was born in 1895 on a homestead in Rock County, Nebraska, in the north-central part of the state. When Hall was five years old, the family moved to Clay Center, Kansas, where she attended Clay Center public schools. Following graduation from high school at the age of 14, she took a job for $5 per week in a Wichita employment agency. Several years later Hall went to work for the father of a friend in Enid, Oklahoma, after which she worked as a stenographer in a bank there.

Not long afterward Hall moved to Kansas City to join the All Night and Day Bank. In 1912 Commerce Trust Company became its receiver, and one of the assets that was transferred to Commerce was Emma Marcus Hall. Her first position was as a secretary in the securities division. During World War I she managed loans and began to specialize in government securities.

She rapidly rose to the position of assistant cashier. In this capacity she bought and sold more bonds than any other woman in the country. During a single day her total trades often exceeded $10 million.

Hall also handled the purchase and sale of stock for the bank's customers. As nominee for the bank, her name appeared on all stocks and bonds traded. But, there was one technicality: the name had to be that of a man. To meet this requirement, Emma Marcus Hall became E. Marcus Hall. This caused some confusion for income tax investigators who could not find a tax form filed by "Mr." Marcus Hall.

Rising up the business ladder from her 1912 entry employment to assistant cashier in 1922, Hall surprised no one when she became the first woman named an assistant vice-president of a Kansas City bank in 1945. A colleague at Commerce said that, "The secret of her success is Miss Hall herself."

Business was her vocation, but after work her avocation of ceramics called her to the home at 4935 Bell Street she shared with her mother. Hall's

COURTESY MISSOURI VALLEY SPECIAL COLLECTIONS, KANSAS CITY PUBLIC LIBRARY, KANSAS CITY, MISSOURI

*Emma Marcus Hall, the first woman to become an assistant vice-president of a Kansas City bank.*

affiliations included the Women's Chamber of Commerce, National Security Traders Association, Bond Traders Club of Kansas City, and Woman's City Club. She was recognized as the city's leading businesswoman in banking.

# JEAN HARLOW
## *Harlean Carpenter*

JEAN HARLOW, THE BLOND bombshell, was dead. No one could believe that Hollywood's most glamorous star was dead at the age of 26.

Born on March 3, 1911, in a house at 3344 Olive Street, Harlean Carpenter was the daughter of Dr. and Mrs. Mont Clair Carpenter. Her first name was taken from the first syllables of her mother's maiden name, Jean Harlow. She was a beautiful blond, blue-eyed baby. The family moved to 4409 Gillham Road and then to a large stone house at 1312 East Seventy-ninth Street. While living there, Harlean attended Miss Barstow's School at 15 Westport Road.

A seemingly idyllic family life came to an end in 1922 when Dr. Carpenter sued his wife for divorce. Shattered by this turn of events, Mrs. Carpenter, an aspiring actress, and her daughter moved to Hollywood in hopes that one of them might catch the eye of a casting director. Harlean attended the Hollywood School for Girls. When no career materialized, the two returned to Kansas City.

Mrs. Carpenter remarried and moved to Chicago. Harlean Carpenter's formal education ended at 16 when she eloped with Charles F. McGrew II. They were divorced two years later.

During this brief marriage Harlean decided to accompany a guest in her home to a screen test. Offered the opportunity to take one herself, she agreed and quickly chose to assume her mother's maiden name, Jean Harlow. The screen test was a huge success. She was on her way.

Her mother was the dominant figure in her life. Every move in Jean Harlow's movie career was discussed daily with her mother,

*Jean Harlow*

and no move, either personal or professional, was made without her approval. No man was ever as important to her.

At first, the best movie roles Jean Harlow could get were bit parts. But, in 1930 Howard Hughes was looking for a replacement for Greta Nissen in his remake of *Hell's Angels* when he found Harlow. She became a star overnight.

Her screen successes were enormous: *Bombshell*, *The Public Enemy* with James Cagney, and *Dinner at Eight* with Marie Dressler and the Barrymores. She was the platinum blond glamour girl of the big screen. But, she wanted more, recognition as an actress rather than just a sex symbol.

Her relationships with men were full of heartache. Harlow's first marriage was over before she was 20 years old, her second ended when her film executive husband committed suicide, and by the end of 1933 she was suing her third husband for divorce.

Only her mother and actor William Powell, also from Kansas City, were at her bedside when she died on June 7, 1937, of uremic poisoning. Two days later she was buried with Hollywood pomp at Forest Lawn Cemetery. Her coffin was blanketed with 1,500 lilies of the valley and 500 gardenias, Clark Gable was a pallbearer, and Jeanette MacDonald and Nelson Eddy sang. And someone left a single gardenia with an unsigned card that read, "Good night, my dearest darling." The platinum blond was dead at 26.

# ANNE HAYES
## Clara Fischer Witt

IN THE EARLY DAYS of radio and television, men held nearly all the on-air positions. This fact did not deter Anne Hayes.

Born Clara Fischer in Brooklyn, New York, on September 15, 1891, she was four years old when her mother died. Her father was a tailor. She came to Kansas City as the 16-year-old bride of Harold W. Witt, a physician on the staff of Osteopathic Hospital.

A totally self-taught broadcaster, her first job was doing a woman's program on KWKC, a small radio station at Thirty-ninth and Main streets that later became KCMO. In 1922 she moved to WDAF, owned by *The Kansas City Star*. Its studio was in the newspaper building at Eighteenth Street and Grand Avenue. Clara Witt, known professionally as Anne Hayes, remained with WDAF until 1935 when she joined KCMO.

Early in her career Anne Hayes demonstrated she knew what women wanted to hear on radio. Her popular 15-minute weekday program, "Today's Woman," had an informal interview format that featured movie stars, royalty, United Nations delegates, teachers, farm women, and others of interest to her audience. Hayes became director of women's activities for KCMO. In 1953 she joined KCMO-TV and started her own show that had the same format as her radio show.

Hayes' work was not confined to broadcasting for she was active in several career-related organizations. In 1950 the Missouri Federation of Women's Clubs chose her as Missouri's outstanding clubwoman. That same year she was elected a director of the Fashion Group, Inc., later becoming its president. An active member of the board of directors of the Women's Chamber of Commerce, she conducted monthly radio programs devoted solely to the organization. For this support she was chosen the first honorary member of the American Business Women's Association in 1953.

In 1949 she was one of 13 women appointed to a national committee of women broadcasters that advised the United Nations Radio Committee. Anne Hayes was elected president of the Heart of America chapter

*Anne Hayes*

COURTESY LILLIAN D. WITT

of Women in Radio and Television, an organization she founded in 1951. American Women in Radio and Television rewarded her accomplishments by naming her national chairman of its public relations committee. In 1963 the Radio and Television Council of Greater Kansas City named her Broadcaster of the Year, and the Kansas City chapter of American Women in Radio and Television designated Hayes as Woman of the Year.

A mandatory retirement policy ended her career in 1957. At that time she was director of women's activities for KCMO and KCMO-TV. Clara Fischer Witt, known to thousands as Anne Hayes, died December 17, 1986, at the age of 95.

# HELEN ROWE HENZE

L.R. LIND, PROFESSOR of Latin and Greek at the University of Kansas, wrote: "Long known as a Kansas City poet and a lover of the classics, Helen Rowe Henze has produced what I regard as the best version of Horace's odes yet made within the stern limitations set by her goal: an imitation which has the rhythm of the original yet reads like an English poem."

Helen Rowe was born in 1900 in Pittsburgh where her father was the advertising and business manager of the Pittsburgh *Gazette-Times* and *Post-Dispatch*. Her mother was a church

COURTESY ARDIS GLENN

*Helen Rowe Henze*

and concert singer. The family came to Kansas City, and Helen graduated from Westport High School before entering Kansas City Junior College. A marriage ended in divorce.

Helen Rowe Henze went to work as a secretary for the Ash Grove Cement Company. Later she was elected assistant secretary, the first woman in the history of the company to be named an officer. After office hours she sang in the Kansas City Philharmonic chorus and composed poetry. Henze was a member of the Poetry Society of America and the O. Henriettas.

Poetry grew in importance in her life with her works appearing in the *Saturday Evening Post* and *The Washington Post. Song of Life* was her first book of poems. Henze became close friends with Frank Glenn, a local rare book dealer, and his wife Ardis because of their mutual love of literature. Frank Glenn Publishing Co. introduced *Each Man's World,* her second collection of poems, in 1950.

Glenn kept urging Henze to write a book of love poems, and she kept declining. Then she had a change of heart. She wrote to Glenn after completing the work: "I am having a case of nerves, I guess . . . now that it has in some way been written through me—I still feel that it is bigger than I am; and it frightens me! . . . How could I, how could anybody have written it? I am torn between eagerness and dread of publication; but it must be published, of course!" *Strange Is the Heart,* 52 sonnets about an unhappy love affair told from the woman's perspective, came out in the fall of 1951. *Arise, My Love,* published by Doubleday & Company in 1953, received national acclaim. Henze's real challenge was yet to come.

Because of her impressive body of works, Dr. D. Herbert Abel, professor of classical languages at Loyola University, paid a visit to Henze. He read to her a smattering of Horace's odes written in Latin two thousand years before, and she was charmed. Intrigued by the meter and content, Henze undertook a translation of the odes with the original meter and alliteration. Armed with Latin dictionaries and grammars as well as Abel's assistance and critiques, she, who had studied just four years of Latin in high school, began the task.

*The Odes of Horace,* translated by Helen Rowe Henze, was published in 1961 by the University of Oklahoma-Norman. Accolades showered in from the academic community as well as requests for additional translations. She declined. "If I had known six years ago of the relentless discipline this was to require, I wonder whether I would have tried it. I never worked so hard on anything, but the work was done *through* me, rather than *by* me. It is a miracle, and I am somewhat dazed that I was permitted to have a part in it."

Helen Rowe Henze died on March 16, 1973.

# ROSA MAY JONES HIBBARD

Rosa May Jones Hibbard died just months before the following words were spoken at the 25th anniversary celebration of the founding of the Jackson County Medical Society library. Logan Clendening, a well-known local physician, expressed the organization's sentiments: "We feel that the success and the enormous service the library has performed is due entirely to [Hibbard's] discrimination and well-planned efforts, which have made it one of the most important medical libraries in the United States. My own memory is filled with numerous instances of her kindness and helpful services."

Rosa May Jones was born in Emporia, Kansas, in 1871, one of six children of Isaiah and Sarah Jones. She grew up watching an almost endless procession of prairie schooners move along

COURTESY METROPOLITAN MEDICAL SOCIETY OF KANSAS CITY

*Rosa May Jones Hibbard*

the Santa Fe Trail. Privation and hardship were a way of life and may have developed what friends later described as her noble and courageous character, attributes that proved invaluable to her as an adult.

Educated in Emporia public schools, she completed her studies at the Emporia Teachers College in the mid-1890s. In February 1897, she married Dr. Harry L. Hibbard, and they came to Kansas City. Widowed just five years later, she returned to her hometown and again enrolled at Emporia Teachers College to obtain advanced library training. In 1904 she became assistant state librarian in Topeka, a position she held for nearly eight years.

The opportunity of a lifetime came in 1912 when she was invited by a group of Kansas City doctors to establish the Kansas City Medical Library. What was started on a shoestring and consisted of a small collection became one of the best medical libraries in the country. Dr. Robert Schauffler spoke for his fellow physicians, Drs. E.H. Skinner, Jabez N. Jackson, and Howard Hill: "We had very little money, and even less library experience, but we had Rosa May Hibbard! And she was an army in herself. I can see her now, going from office to office, collecting books and journals and reprints, carrying them home in her hands. Many a time I have told her that when she popped her head into a doctor's sanctum none of his literary property was safe. Sooner or later she would succeed in making off with it. And how the library grew!"

In 1920 it became a part of the Jackson County Medical Society. Hibbard was named the executive secretary as well as librarian of the organization.

The library was unique for many reasons: it began with a librarian first; it never had an endowment or capital funds; and its support was through membership dues that did not exceed $10 per year. Housed in donated space in the Rialto Building for several years, it was moved many times during Hibbard's tenure.

Hibbard's dream was to make it the largest and most complete medical library in America. Many feel she succeeded.

Rosa May Hibbard died on June 2, 1937, on board a train returning from a convention of medical librarians. Burial was in Emporia.

# OPAL TROUT HILL

I F I'M GOING TO DIE, I might as well do it on a golf practice tee," she quipped as she neared her eightieth birthday. Forty-eight years earlier her doctors had sadly pronounced that she was a victim of an incurable kidney infection, complicated by anemia, and had only three years to live. But Opal Trout Hill not only defied the predictions but also outlived the predictors.

Born June 2, 1892, in Nebraska, she and her family soon moved to Minneapolis, Kansas, after her father died. She grew up knowing the meaning of hard work and responsibility. During high school she took care of her ailing mother and found she had an aptitude for nursing. After high school she applied for admission to the nursing school of Swedish Lutheran Hospital (now Trinity Lutheran Hospital), but "Dr. Outland pooh-poohed the idea, believing I was too young." Opal convinced him she was ready, entered the program, and graduated two years later. She met her future husband, Oscar Stuart Hill, a prominent Kansas City lawyer, when he was a patient and she a nurse at the hospital.

After the birth of their son Stuart, severe health problems developed. Ignoring the well-meaning prophets of doom, she decided to take the only encouraging medical advice, which was offered by Dr. Franklin D. Murphy. His prescription was sunshine and fresh air, so at the age of 31 years Opal Hill

COURTESY MRS. STUART B. HILL

*Opal Trout Hill in 1928 when she won an important tournament in Miami Beach, Florida.*

headed for the golf course. She recollected that she knew very little about the game.

She worked at golf with the same dedication and ability she approached nursing. Soon fellow members of Meadow Lake Country Club at Seventy-fifth Street and State Line Road became aware of her presence. At her first tournament in 1923, to which she was encouraged to enter because the $2 entry fees were sorely needed, she shot a 142 for 18 holes. Determined to improve, she took lessons from the club professional, Al Lesperance. "I would practice for three hours at a time on one shot, never quitting it until it satisfied me and my trainer. He criticized everything unmercifully, my stance, my pivot, my swing. He used to say, 'If you can stand my gaff, I'll make a medalist out of you.'" Lesperance knew what he was talking about: two years later Opal Hill won the women's city title.

By 1928 she had captured three major amateur titles. "A champion," she said, "outplays others by determination and desire—by always going a bit beyond." Before she quit tournament play, she had won more than 250 trophies. Her wins included 14 consecutive Kansas City Women's championships, 3 Missouri State Amateur titles, 3 Women's Western Amateur championships, 3 Western Open crowns, and 4 Trans-Mississippi titles. She was a member of the first three Curtis Cup teams and, in fact, helped launch the international event when in 1930 she and a group of women participated in a series of match plays in England. In 1937 she set a course record at Indian Hills Country Club with a 12-under-par 66 during the

*Opal Trout Hill*

Missouri Amateur competition. She shot a hole in one on the third hitting from the men's tee. This record stood for 12 years.

Opal Hill turned professional in 1938. She and Helen Hicks were the only two women golf pros in the world, and they helped organize a group that became the Ladies Professional Golf Association (LPGA). Her golfing feats are documented in a display at the Golf House, home of the U.S. Golf Association Museum and Library at Far Hills, New Jersey.

In her later years she gave golf lessons. At the age of 80 she taught six hours a day, six days a week during the summer. By then she was plagued with arthritis, but she still shot in the 80s!

Opal Hill died on June 23, 1981, and was remembered by Joe McGuff as "probably the most remarkable athlete in the history of women's golf. . . . She was a woman of rare spirit and courage. In life or on the golf course, Opal Hill did not like to lose."

# VASSIE JAMES WARD HILL

VASSIE JAMES WARD simply wanted to do the best for her children. What she did was found Country Day School for boys and Sunset Hill School for girls and thus introduce progressive and experimental ideas in education to Kansas City.

She was born on March 29, 1875, the eldest of five children of John Crawford and Fanny Shouse James. After leaving Central High School, she received a degree from Vassar College, her mother's alma mater. Soon after, on October 26, 1898, she married Hugh C. Ward, son of Indian trader and trapper Seth Ward. In 1870 Seth Ward had purchased over 200 acres from William Bent, another well-known trader, and built a residence that is still standing at 1032 West Fifty-fifth Street.

Three sons and one daughter were born during their marriage. After her husband died in 1909, Vassie Ward took over the reins of the Ward Investment Company, which had been established in 1902. The Sunset Hill area, a portion of the original Bent-Ward property, was developed by Vassie Ward and the company.

She considered the welfare and education of her children to be

of the utmost importance. Wanting only the very best, she opened
the Kansas City Country Day School for boys in 1910. Vassie Ward
implemented several new ideas that were then being used by only a
half dozen Eastern boarding schools: stringent curriculum, rest peri-
ods, hot lunches, organized athletics, and leisure time filled with
activities. Country Day School was so successful that Mrs. William
F. Patton, Mrs. Justin D. Bowersock, and a few of their friends asked
Vassie Ward to open a similar school for girls. Sunset Hill School for
girls began in Ward's Sunset Drive home in 1913.

An ardent Democrat, in 1919 Vassie Ward became the first
woman from Missouri ever to be elected a member of the Democratic National Committee, the same year she married Dr. A. Ross Hill,
president of the University of Missouri. Additionally in 1919 she
became one of just five women appointed to study and promote the
interests of women in connection with deliberations of the World
War I peace conference and the League of Nations. She later helped
found the Jefferson Democratic Club, was an active member of the
Missouri League of Women Voters, and was elected president of the
Kansas City League of
Women Voters. In 1933
Eleanor Roosevelt appointed
her chairman of the National Women's Committee for
Mobilization for Human
Need. Her interest in chil-
dren led her to join Mary
Harmon Weeks, founder of
the parent-teacher move-
ment, in establishing the
Kansas City Children's
Bureau in 1936 when Weeks
was 89 years old.

*Vassie James Ward Hill*

Vassie James Ward Hill
died June 23, 1954, leaving a
legacy in the field of private
education that thrives today
as Pembroke Hill School.
Burial was at Mount Wash-
ington Cemetery.

# KATE HINKLE

IN 1908 A VERY determined woman bought two wooden tubs with a portion of the sum total of her capital, $8, and launched Kansas City's first French laundry.

Needing to earn a living following her husband's death, Kate Hinkle turned to what she knew best: the care of fine laces, priceless linens, and exquisite embroideries. When she had worked as a children's nurse, she deplored the many pieces that were discarded because of poor laundering. She knew she could do better.

The first customers of Kate Hinkle's French Laundry were former employers living along Armour Boulevard or in the vicinity of Forty-fourth Street from Warwick Boulevard to Oak Street. She was asked to work on their daughters' bridal trousseaux. Hinkle went into their homes to launder the linens and embroidered articles of the brides-to-be. In those days many brides had an abundance of French embroidered pieces and household linens that required laundering.

Since Kansas Citians were accustomed to sending their fine laces and linens to New York City or other places in the East, Hinkle's business was not an overnight success. Time was required for people to realize the quality of her operation, but she was firm in her belief that she did the best work.

She pushed a cart making pickups and deliveries with her ever-present Irish smile. Work was being done at her home. It was truly handwork with wooden tubs, washboards, and padded tables for ironing.

The business prospered and grew. Hinkle moved from her home to a rented building on Gillham Road near Linwood Boulevard and finally into a brick building she had

COURTESY MISSOURI VALLEY SPECIAL COLLECTIONS, KANSAS CITY PUBLIC LIBRARY, KANSAS CITY, MO

*Kate Hinkle*

constructed at 3121 Gillham Road where she employed 30 women to wash and iron and had two delivery trucks.

Her customers were located from Washington, D.C., to Los Angeles, from North Dakota to Texas with the heaviest concentration in Missouri, Kansas, Oklahoma, and Texas. For many years her customers relied on her mastery to launder their laces, lingerie, linen napery, quilts, and christening robes. Her work was always done by hand; the only machine used was a huge centrifugal wringer that gently squeezed water out of material.

Fine washing was her pride. Hinkle retained her enthusiasm and desire and saved the biggest problems for herself. Once she was asked to launder a damask tablecloth owned by William Rockhill Nelson that was worth several thousand dollars. She worked on the eight-yard-long piece by herself. Hinkle said that her most difficult job was washing an embroidered 90-inch round tablecloth made in a French convent. She remembered, "Well, this cloth was so fine and the embroidery so heavy that when I took it out of the water, it looked just like a bird's nest." She let the material almost dry before ironing and learned a valuable lesson in the process.

Kate Hinkle, laundress of national note, died on December 11, 1931, at her home above Kate Hinkle's French Laundry. She was 55 years old.

# MARY ROCKWELL HOOK

ACCORDING TO Mary Rockwell Hook she entered a world "where women were compelled to slay tradition in order to mount their professions." She had to do her fair share when she entered the male-dominated field of architecture.

Born on September 8, 1877, in Junction City, Kansas, she was the third of five daughters of Bertrand and Julia Rockwell. Her father, a captain in the Union Army during the Civil War, had made his fortune in grain and banking. Mary Rockwell was sent to Dana Hall, a four-year preparatory school in Wellesley, Massachusetts, and then Wellesley College from which she graduated in 1900.

Captain Rockwell took his family on trips to Europe and the Far

East. It was in the Philippines that Mary Rockwell made her decision to become an architect. Recalling the American consulate, she wrote, "Someone needed to improve the design of buildings used by our government abroad. I made up my mind to go home and study architecture."

In 1903 she enrolled in architecture in the School of the Art Institute of Chicago. She was the only woman in her class. Two years later she left for Paris to study with Marcel Auburtin; again she was the sole female student.

When the family moved to Kansas City, she experienced discrimination in hiring on a personal level. When she applied for a position with Wilder and Wight, a well-known architectural firm, she was turned down because "we can't swear at women and they can't climb all over full-sized details." Undaunted by this rejection, Mary Rockwell continued seeking employment and was hired by the firm of Howe, Hoit and Cutler. She remained with the firm for one year.

Mary Rockwell's first commission was awarded by her father in 1908. She designed a house near Fifty-third Terrace and Brookside Boulevard. Several out-of-town commissions followed as well as another family home, this one at 1004 West Fifty-second Street. The home had long porches at each end where she would awaken on summer mornings to a wonderful view of the polo field at the Kansas City Country Club (now Loose Park). The houses she designed reflected her love of nature.

*Mary Rockwell Hook*

The Pine County Settlement School in Harlan County, Kentucky, built in 1913, was one of her few nonresidential projects.

Rockwell was an early recycler, a preservationist of materials used in older buildings. In the Fifty-second Street home she used a fireplace from her Aunt Katie Clarke's house at 1016 Central Street, two-story factory windows, wooden beams from an old railroad bridge across the Kansas River, and staircase paneling from a house that had been demolished to make way for the Hotel Bellerive.

She and Mac Remington formed an architectural firm in 1923 and were kept busy designing elegant homes in Kansas City and across the country. Those in Kansas City are still among the city's finest.

At the age of 44 she took time out from work to marry Inghram Hook, a prominent Kansas City lawyer. Her father's fortune and her husband's law practice made her financially secure and therefore not dependent upon her business for income.

By 1925 she had established her ability to site homes on hillsides. Vassie Ward Hill, president of Ward Investment Company, asked her to design a house on a bluff just south of Brush Creek at Sunset Drive and Rockwell Lane. She succeeded and produced an elegant home that is testament to her skill. Mary Rockwell Hook's Sunset Hill houses are her monument.

In her later years, she wrote, "Now that I am blind, I spend my days listening to the wonderful recording of books . . . In the waking hours of my nights, I spend on imaginative designs. Among other things I have even located and planned a new capitol for France!" Mary Rockwell Hook died on September 8, 1978, on her 101st birthday. She was buried in Mount Washington Cemetery.

# ADA HOOVER

S HE ROLLED HER OWN—pills, that is—in the days before pharmaceutical houses supplied them to pharmacies.

Ada Hoover came to Kansas City from Mansfield, a small town in southern Missouri, with one goal in mind: to study pharmacy. Her work in a hometown drugstore during her high school years had whetted her desire for this career.

Entering the College of Pharmacy in 1907, she found herself the only woman in a class of 75 even though she had been promised there would be other women. Completing the two-year course, she became one of the first women to be licensed as a pharmacist in the state of Missouri. With her diploma tucked under her arm, she applied at the Hugo A. Brecklein Pharmacy which had opened in 1895 at 904 Grand Avenue. She recalled that, "He was dubious about employing a woman pharmacist and said he would think it over. That night I received a special delivery letter . . . that told me to report the next day." She did and remained on the job for over 50 years.

Her work carried enormous responsibility. Doctors prescribed medications, and Hoover had to measure, mix, and grind the ingredients with a mortar and pestle. She used a small machine to round out the pills before applying a smooth glaze.

In 1943 Ada Hoover bought Brecklein's interest in the business. She operated the pharmacy in partnership with Joseph H. Brecklein, Hugo's son, for a number of years.

# ROSE SHKLAR MINDLIN JACOBSON

A MATERNAL INSTINCT TO provide for three small sons led to the founding of one of Kansas City's leading women's clothing stores, Mindlin's.

Rose Shklar was born in Russia about 1877. Her father worked for the czar purchasing tracts of forest land. When Rose was 11 years old, her family came to America and settled in Barber County, Kansas, near Kiowa. She was educated in a rural one-room schoolhouse and, while still a student, taught the younger children.

When the U.S. government opened Oklahoma to settlement during the late 1880s, Rose's father and brother were ill so she was sent to stake out the family claim. This was quite a feat for a teenage girl, but she was strong enough to hold her own in the melee of the land rush.

During a trip to Chicago, Rose met her future husband, Barnett Mindlin. They were married in 1896 and moved to Kansas City in 1902. He operated a jewelry store near Twelfth Street and Grand Avenue until his death in 1923. By 1904 they were parents of Harold, David, and Ernest Mindlin. Rose Mindlin's primary concern was to provide food, shelter, and clothing for them, but she had no business experience other than teaching. She did, however, like people and people liked her. And they loved the hats she made and wore.

With her small savings she bought materials,

*Rose Shklar Mindlin Jacobson*

COURTESY STAN MINDLIN

hired a couple of employees, and in 1904 began making and selling hats in a small shop at 1012 East Twelfth Street. Businessmen scoffed at the residential location, predicting a quick failure since it was so far from the downtown retail area, but it proved to be a wise choice. It was in the middle of the carriage trade, and women in the area could afford to pay $150 for just the right hat. Living quarters in the rear of the shop allowed Rose Mindlin to keep an eye on her boys.

After World War I, her customers moved south to homes along The Paseo, Armour Boulevard, and Warwick Boulevard, and she followed them. In 1918 her new store at 3221 Troost Avenue opened and was the first specialty store in the area.

Her son Harold had been working for her and in 1922 was made a partner in the business. The Flapper Era was beginning and styles were changing. Harold realized that the store needed more than hats so women's ready-to-wear apparel was introduced. Mindlin's was opened downtown in 1929 at 1109 Walnut Street and in 1940 was moved to a larger space at 1014 Walnut.

The suburbs became an important retail market, and to keep pace the family opened a new Mindlin's, the first women's specialty shop on the Country Club Plaza.

In 1936 Rose Mindlin married Abe Jacobson, a Topeka real estate investor. Shortly after their marriage she retired from active participation in the clothing business but never lost interest in it. Her three sons assumed control.

Rose Shklar Mindlin Jacobson died on June 14, 1951. She was buried at Rose Hill Cemetery.

COURTESY STAN MINDLIN

*Rose Shklar Mindlin Jacobson*

# ANNA D. JONES

THE NAME ON THE glass door of Room 404 in the Scarritt Building at 818 Grand Avenue read *A.D. Jones, Customs Broker.* Jones had served the city and the Midwest for over 18 years as the intermediary between the United States government and importers of goods from foreign countries. A.D. Jones was a big man in the business— or to put it more correctly, a big woman. Anna D. Jones was believed to be the only female customs broker in the country.

Finding herself a widow with a son to support, Jones was forced to go to work. She later ascribed entering her profession to good luck: "I just drifted into this business, going into it in a small way at first, never dreaming that it would develop into a large business."

Customs brokerage was difficult to learn since federal regulations frequently changed and were always wrapped in governmental red tape. Additionally, Jones had to know the customs and tax laws of other countries. One invoice from Kobe, Japan, filled 40 pages and was written entirely in Japanese with the estimated value in yen. When a shipment reached Kansas City, Jones determined its value, submitted her estimate of the duty to a government customs officer, agreed on a figure, paid the duty on behalf of her client, and arranged for the shipment to be removed from the government warehouse. The duty on one shipment of Japanese floor matting amounted to $18,000. Jones paid in cash.

In a 1914 interview, she stated, "There is no lawyer in the city I know of who has knowledge of the customs laws which are very intricate. So I had to study up on those laws for myself and master

*Anna D. Jones*

COURTESY MISSOURI VALLEY SPECIAL COLLECTIONS, KANSAS CITY PUBLIC LIBRARY, KANSAS CITY, MO them." Master them she did, for her business became so successful that she employed her own agents in many countries.

Anna D. Jones climbed to the top of the customs brokerage ladder handling articles ranging from puppies to mummies and zinc ore to hatpins. Her dream was "to see the Kansas City port of entry become the headquarters for this trade district instead of St. Louis. I am constantly working toward that end."

# LOUISA POTEET JOHNSTON

S HE WAS A WIRY and tenacious woman who was completely focused on creating a memorial park around the old house at 8145 State Line Road. It was not just any old house but that built in 1856 by Alexander Majors, Louisa Poteet Johnston's great-grandfather. It was the only extant headquarters of the Santa Fe freighting operations of Russell, Majors and Waddell Transportation Company. Majors was co-founder of the Pony Express, a remarkable venture that failed within 18 months of its inception and bankrupted the firm.

Louisa (her preferred pronunciation was *Lou-eye-sa*) Poteet Johnston was born on July 30, 1890, the daughter of William Barnett Johnston, a descendant of an early Jackson County family, and Susan A. Simpson, granddaughter of Majors. Her dream was to establish a park around her great-grandfather's house not only as a monument to

COURTESY ALEXANDER MAJORS HISTORICAL SOCIETY

*Louisa Poteet Johnston*

him but also to the transportation company that helped develop the West by supplying forts and settlements with its network of freight wagons. Majors became one of Kansas City's first millionaires but died bankrupt in 1900. Although she remembered little of him since she was only ten years old when he died, she learned all there was to know about him when she was an adult.

Johnston was a teacher in Kansas City public schools. In the 1930s she taught shorthand and typing at East High School and later mathematics and typing at Westport High School. Reportedly she lost her teaching position for publicly urging the United States to give aid to its allies before Pearl Harbor. When she ignored requests to remain silent, the school administration fired her. For a short time she was the registrar at Mills College in Oakland, California.

Johnston felt she had to own and preserve the old family home. Although it had survived a number of owners, a real threat arose in 1925 when the Kansas City Board of Education bought it, used it as a school for three years, and then decided to demolish it to make way for a new school. But the old Majors home refused to fall before the wrecking ball (the new school was built at Eighty-first and Mercier streets). Louisa Johnston bought the derelict house in 1935. Its windows were broken, chimneys crumbling, doors missing, and the roof needed repairs, but she moved in anyway and began doing what she could on her meager salary. In 1941 she lived with three cats, four dogs, and twenty goats in only three of the home's eleven rooms.

Too busy and independent to consider marriage, she spent her evening hours writing and telephoning anyone she felt she could persuade to support preserving the house. Originally she envisioned a 40-acre memorial park but by 1968 was willing to settle for 22 acres. (The house now sits on 1.1 acres.)

Life became increasingly difficult as Johnston's funds diminished. In 1969 she fell on ice outside her home and suffered a broken hip. When she was released from the hospital, she returned not to the big house, since it was filled with her collection of newspapers and magazines, but to the little house behind it.

She died on March 10, 1979, in that cottage. The Alexander Majors Historical House stands as a tribute to the tenacity, love, and sacrifice of Louisa Poteet Johnston.

# MILDRED KAUFFMAN

S HE MADE A CAREER of doing what she loved best: flying. It was how Mildred Kauffman made her living and also how she died.

Mildred Kauffman, who lived with her parents, Mr. and Mrs. Josiah Kauffman, at 3130 Jefferson Street, was a nationally known Kansas City aviatrix and licensed transport pilot. In 1930 she passed the requirements for the highest license issued to pilots by the aeronautic board of the Department of Commerce. Kauffman was the only woman in the area with such a rating and one of only a few women in the nation to be rated by the government as a transport pilot. She held the women's world record of performing 46 consecutive loops in 1930.

Tragedy struck early Sunday evening, August 7, 1932. Kauffman took off in a monoplane from the Kansas City Municipal Airport with Russell Shaw as passenger. About 20 minutes later Don Moss, piloting a biplane, took off from the Fairfax Airport with 12-year-old passenger Jack Leftwich.

To the absolute horror of a large crowd assembled to watch the activities at the airport, the planes collided at top speed, locking wings and plummeting to the ground at the north end of Fairfax Airport. Shaw later reported that Kauffman saw the other plane too late. "She made a last desperate effort to save us by zooming her ship almost straight up." Spectators jumped into their automobiles and sped to the crash site where Moss had pulled the victims from the wreckage. All but Kauffman suffered only minor injuries. She died early the next morning at the age of 25.

# CLARA E. KELLOGG

IT WAS NOT ALWAYS a society magazine. "When we bought it, we wanted to reform everything . . . deplorable conditions, civic and otherwise, in Kansas City. But later we decided we couldn't go on with our reform, that people didn't want to be reformed anyway, at least by us. They wanted to be amused, and that's what we have been trying to do ever since." So spoke Clara E. Kellogg, who with her friend and partner Katherine Baxter bought *The Independent* on January 1, 1909.

Born in Ohio, Kellogg was lured to Kansas City in 1902 from her real estate business in the East by her brother Frederick W. Kellogg, who had acquired the *Kansas City World* newspaper in 1897. Clara Kellogg joined the staff and met Katherine Baxter.

When the paper was sold in 1905, the two women went to St. Joseph and pooled their funds so that they could found the *St. Joseph Star*. Kellogg was in charge of the business and publishing side of the operation while Baxter acted as the society and Sunday editor. In a very short time the paper earned a profit. When an opportunity to sell presented itself, they sold. Returning to Kansas City, the two edited a short-lived monthly paper called *The Butterfly*.

*Clara E. Kellogg*

Undaunted by the lack of any long-term success, their next venture was to establish the Kellogg-Baxter Printing Company, the first of its type to be solely owned and operated by women in Kansas City. Fascinated with the mechanics of printing, Kellogg learned to set type and feed the presses.

Their big opportunity came and they grabbed it.

Scraping together sufficient funds, Kellogg and Baxter bought *The Independent* from George Creel on January 1, 1909. They had found their niche.

Baxter assumed responsibility for the editorial content while Kellogg handled the business end of the operation. They both quickly concluded that their readers were uninterested in civic reform but wanted to be entertained with what was going on in society.

Kellogg and Baxter continued their profitable partnership. By 1928 the magazine's circulation was over 4,500. "We were never in the red nor in all of the time had a cross word," Kellogg said. "Even two fires have not set us back an issue of the magazine."

After Baxter died on April 4, 1924, Kellogg managed *The Independent* until she sold it to Mrs. Gleed Gaylord in 1939. Clara E. Kellogg died at her home at 1837 Pendleton Avenue on January 7, 1944.

# ENID JACKSON KEMPER

HER DAYS USUALLY began at 6 A.M. and progressed through a maze of community meetings. "Sometimes," she mused, "I'm made chairman, but more often treasurer of the groups and projects I assist—probably because I am a banker's wife." That was far too modest an assessment because Enid Jackson Kemper had all the necessary skills to excel in every position she held.

Enid Ann Jackson was born on June 12, 1897, in Victoria, British Columbia, the daughter of Robert G. and Robena Jackson. When her father, a physician, was hired by the Jefferson Medical College, the family accompanied him to Philadelphia. They later moved to San Francisco and then Tacoma. After graduating from Ogontz School in Pennsylvania, Jackson joined the motor corps in World War I as an emergency aid driver.

Following the war, she returned to Tacoma to begin a newspaper career. Jackson entered the male-dominated profession as the *Tacoma Tribune*'s society editor. "I took the job, and I had a terrible time at first, because in those days women just didn't work on

*Enid Jackson Kemper*

newspapers. The men were determined to make it unpleasant for me so I would leave, but I stayed." She finally earned their approval by working all night during an election coverage. When morning came, she was invited to join the reporters for breakfast. Jackson earned a byline as a movie reviewer during her one-year newspaper career.

While on a trip to Florida in 1920, Jackson stopped in Kansas City for a visit and met Rufus Crosby Kemper. Six months later, on April 20, 1921, they were married.

For a period of time Enid Kemper's life was focused on rearing their three children with spare moments spent on golf and gardening. She was one of the original members of the Westport Garden Club, an organization of women that beautified Kansas City through a variety of projects.

Kemper became involved with numerous causes and organizations in the city. She served as the chairman of the Red Cross Nurses Aides during World War II. As an active member of the Junior League of Kansas City, Missouri, she worked on the Cowtown Carnival to raise funds for the American Royal. The Kansas City Art Institute, St. Andrew's Episcopal Church, St. Luke's Hospital, Cancer Fund, and United Fund were enriched by her fund-raising skills. The Enid and Crosby Kemper Foundation, which was formed in 1973, has generously supported a broad range of activities in the area.

She was known and admired for doing her homework on civic projects. Her accomplishments led to her appointment as secretary of the Lay Citizens' Advisory Commission of the Kansas City Board of Education in 1950.

Kemper is probably best known as a co-founder with Clara Stager Hockaday of the Jewel Ball which began in 1954 to raise funds for the Kansas City Philharmonic Orchestra. It was the first event of its kind to be held at the Nelson-Atkins Museum of Art. For three years Kemper was its chairman; in 1957 she was named honorary chairman and head of the advisory board.

Enid Jackson Kemper died January 1, 1979. During her lifetime she made invaluable contributions to many community efforts.

# DELLA COCHRANE LAMB

WHEN ONLY A TEENAGER, Della Cochrane began doing mission work caring for infants. Sadly, this woman who loved babies so much was to see both of her own children die.

Born in Bloomington, Illinois, Della Cochrane moved to 1807 East Seventh Street in Kansas City with her family. Her father, Luman H. Cochrane, operated a fruit produce business at the City Market. The Methodist church several blocks from where they lived, opened a day nursery in a brick house on Fifth Street for children of working mothers in the 1890s. One of the first volunteers to join the staff was Della Cochrane. This marked the beginning of a lifetime of community work that would earn her national recognition.

Her home base was the Institutional Church located at 702 Admiral Boulevard. It was formed as an outgrowth of the day nursery she had served.

Della married Colonel Fred A. Lamb, a former Kansas City police commissioner who also served in the Third Regiment of the Missouri National Guard. His dedication to the service of underprivileged children equaled that of his wife. In 1937 as Colonel Lamb was returning with his wife from a summer camp for children, an automobile accident ended his life. This tragedy together with the deaths of their two children was a tremendous test of Della Lamb's faith. It never wavered. In fact, her devotion to the well-being of children only seemed to grow.

The Institutional Neighborhood House, with its origins in the Fifth Street day nursery, opened in 1906, and Lamb was president of its board of directors for 27 years. Its 20 rooms housed one of

*Della Cochrane Lamb*

COURTESY DELLA C. LAMB COMMUNITY SERVICES

Kansas City's first public gymnasiums, a sewing school, night school, summer ice service, kindergarten, mothers' club room, dining room, and playroom. The juvenile court referred neglected children to it for temporary care. In 1946 the name was changed to the Della C. Lamb Neighborhood House.

Lamb gained national prominence among Methodists, serving for eight years as the secretary of the women's division of Christian service which supervised the national operation of neighborhood centers, mountain schools, women's colleges, and mission work. She also participated in the National College for Christian Workers. Through her efforts the college, located at Fifteenth Street and Van Brunt Boulevard, received a $100,000 prayer offering.

Della Cochrane Lamb, a quiet, unobtrusive woman, died January 27, 1951, leaving a legacy of unselfish giving to her church and community.

# JULIA LEE

SHE HAD HER OWN special way of singing the blues. Sometimes she sang troubled blues, other times dirty blues—the kind her mother taught her not to sing—in an earthy, rollicking voice that could drop off to a sound as soft and smooth as velvet.

Born on Halloween of 1902 in Kansas City, Julia Lee was the daughter of George and Kate Lee. She made her singing and piano-playing debut with her father's trio when she was just three years old. Completing Attucks School, she graduated from Lincoln High School in 1917.

A year later Julia Lee began singing and playing the piano in her brother George's band. Members of the band included such luminaries as Count Basie, Hot Lips Page, Ben Webster, Baby Lovett, Chuck Berry, Bennie Moten, and Lester Young. The band gained a national reputation. When it broke up, she teamed with drummer Baby Lovett, and Kansas City musical history was made. They were the stuff of legend. In 1948 Harry Truman invited them to perform at the White House to celebrate his election victory.

Julia Lee spent many years singing and playing in nightclubs

COURTESY JACKSON COUNTY HISTORICAL SOCIETY ARCHIVES

*Julia Lee*

along Twelfth Street and sang at clubs operated by Milton Morris from the early 1930s to 1950. Her fans were sure to hear such favorites as the risque song, "You Gotta Gimme What Ya Got," "King Size Papa," and "Julia Blues." An album recorded with Jay McShann's band on Capitol Records in 1944 brought fame when disc jockeys featured the song "Trouble in Mind."

She married Frank Duncan, star catcher with the Kansas City Monarchs, and had one son.

On December 7, 1958, Julia Lee suffered a fatal heart attack. She was buried at Highland Cemetery.

# EMMA LARD LONGAN

E MMA LARD LONGAN was a lifelong champion of education and equal rights for women. It is not at all surprising that she, the daughter of highly respected minister Moses Easterly Lard who founded Antioch Church at 4805 Antioch Road, had these interests. Her father said he wanted to be remembered as "a believer in the dignity of womanhood at a time when most men regarded women as coy and artful pets, playthings, and toys."

Emma Lard was born in 1855 in Liberty, Missouri, where she received her early education before leaving to attend Hamilton College in Lexington, Kentucky. Shortly after her graduation, she married George Baker Longan whose father was also a minister. Settling in Kansas City, George Longan went to work for the Kansas City School District, distinguishing himself for more than 30 years as a principal and later as superintendent of schools. He died on June 29, 1911.

Parents of three boys, the Longans lived near Eleventh and Cherry streets. Emma Longan wanted her boys to enjoy an outdoor life so they moved to the country—1723 Michigan Avenue. Later the family lived at 3735 Tracy Avenue.

When her children were old enough, Emma Longan turned her attention to the community. She realized that women needed a knowledge of parliamentary law to participate effectively in public life. She founded the Longan Study Club in 1900. The object of the club was the "pro-motion of Intellectu-al Culture, Mutual Helpfulness, and the Study of Parliamen-tary Law." Many prominent women were members.

At a time when men did most of the voting and all of the lawmaking, Longan realized it was vital that parliamentary rules of order be made understandable to women. She did just that by writing *Parliamentary Law Made Easy* in 1909. By 1924 over 200,000 copies of the book had been sold, and Emma Longan was a national authority on the subject.

COURTESY © THE KANSAS CITY STAR COMPANY

*Emma Lard Longan*

Longan along with Phoebe Ess worked diligently to give women the right to vote and a place in government. She succeeded Sarah Coates as president of the Equal Suffrage Association and was one of the first members of the Kansas City chapter of the Women's Christian Temperance Union, served as president of the Council of Women's Clubs for several terms, and was the president of the Christian Women's Board of Missions.

Because of her interest in women and politics, Longan was elected the first woman member of the upper house of the City Council in 1922 as an independent Democrat. Longan noted, "We always have had to fight the bosses, even in our own party." She listened to her conscience not her party leaders when she opposed the abolition of jitneys that many women had to use to get around town. She advocated better schools, better streets, and simplification of city government.

Emma Lard Longan died on May 1, 1924, at her home and was buried at Elmwood Cemetery. The parliamentarian, suffragist, and council member had accomplished much in her 69 years.

# BETTYE WILSON MILLER

SHE WAS KNOWN as the high priestess, the reigning queen of Kansas City jazz. Bettye Wilson Miller's music could be thunderous or lyrical, complex or simple; contrasts were ever-present in the style of this jazz pianist and contralto. If pleased with her own performance, she would end the piece with a throaty laugh.

Bettye Wilson was born into a musical family in Clinton, Missouri, in 1928. She attended Lincoln University in Jefferson City and received a bachelor's and master's degree in vocal music. After two years of elementary school teaching in West Plains, Missouri, she went to Philadelphia in 1946 for further study to develop her contralto voice.

Frustrated in getting concert bookings, she played steadily at clubs in the city. When she came to Kansas City in 1953 with a baby daughter from her first marriage, her true style emerged.

Bettye Miller accepted a three-day contract offered by Ed Schockey, owner of the Golden Horseshoe Lounge at 3243 Troost Avenue. The three days extended into ten years with the Bettye Miller Trio: Bettye played piano, Wallace Jones drums, and Milt Abel bass. Miller and Abel became partners in music and marriage. They were leaders in a style they called "contemporary swing" that revitalized Kansas City jazz with polish and sophistication.

In addition to their superb musical ability was a subtle intimacy evident in their work that brought an extra dimension to their music. "It's a funny thing," she said, "I've got to have room to follow my feelings. A lot of times Milt and I will work out a tune in rehearsal, then I'll tackle it a whole different way at a performance, depending on how I feel. Milt's beautiful; he just comes right on with me no matter how I start off." They played the Dunes Hotel in Las Vegas, Mr. Kelly's in Chicago, the Embers in New York, and Mr. Putsch's and several other clubs in Kansas City to a devoted following. No matter how often they were asked to play "Red Sails in the Sunset," it always sounded fresh, flawless, and entertaining.

Bettye Miller died February 28, 1977. Her death from cancer was a shock to the entire jazz community for she had brought joy to the lives of those who knew her. A special memorial service was held at the Charlie Parker Memorial Foundation to raise funds to defray the costs of her medical bills.

COURTESY © THE KANSAS CITY STAR COMPANY

*Bettye Miller with Milt Abel*

# PATTI MOORE

THE ENTIRE CITY mourned her death. Commanding the respect of everyone who knew her, Patti Moore served as the matron for the Kansas City Police Department for 15 years.

Born in Harrodsburg, Kentucky, in 1834, she was the daughter of Hiram and Katherine Deweese. After she married George W. Moore, a Louisville merchant, at the age of 17, the newlyweds lived in Platte County and St. Joseph before coming to Kansas City. They operated the Tremont House, a fashionable inn located on West Fifth Street until her husband's failing health forced Patti Moore to find a job. Her husband died in 1898.

In 1881 she was appointed manager of the women's department of the expositions and interstate fairs held in Kansas City. Two years later she was honored with an appointment as a commissioner for the 1893 World's Fair in Chicago. However, it was in the role of police matron that Moore made her mark.

COURTESY MISSOURI VALLEY SPECIAL COLLECTIONS, KANSAS CITY PUBLIC LIBRARY, KANSAS CITY, MISSOURI

*Patti Moore*

During the movement to add matrons to police forces, she was appointed to that position on the Kansas City Police Department in 1889. Because she was 55 years old at the time of appointment, the oldest matron in the United States, Moore was chosen president of the Western Association of Police Matrons in 1892.

In one year alone she reported over 6,000 cases were handled by her department, and she dealt personally with almost all of them. In her official capacity she listened to hard-luck stories, gave advice to girls who had gone wrong, told women of the evils of alcohol, consoled heartbroken mothers and wives, and helped the needy. Kansas City Police Chief Hayes said at her funeral, "She was a woman who had always fought for the uplifting of her sex among the criminal classes and had saved many a wayward girl from a life of shame."

Steadfast in her belief that alcohol was the product of the devil, she was a longtime member of the Women's Christian Temperance Union (WCTU). In fact, it was partially due to the suggestion of the local chapter that she received the position of matron.

In February 1904, Moore was taken ill and never fully recovered. She was forced to direct most of her work from her quarters at the police department until early in November when she suffered a heart attack. Moore died at the Red Cross Hospital on November 17, 1904. She was the mother of ten children, only one of whom was living at the time of her death.

An escort of honor made up of members of the police department, the United Confederate Veterans, and the Daughters of the Confederacy accompanied the body from the church to Union Cemetery.

# ANNA M. NEARING

FIRST-TIME AND experienced travelers alike found entering the cavernous Kansas City Union Station an awesome and often frightening experience. The Grand Hall or lobby measured 240' x 100' with 90' ceilings. There was also a huge 450' x 120' waiting room that stood above the maze of railroad tracks. But in the station there was a haven, a place filled with compassion and answers.

From the day the Union Station opened with a 21-gun salute in November 1914, it was a hubbub of activity. Bewildered travelers, bleary-eyed, weary, and sometimes lost were revived and sent on their way by Anna M. Nearing, who for over 21 years served as the matron of Union Station.

Born in Toledo, Ohio, Nearing moved with her family to Kansas City in 1890. Her father, Edward Robert Atwill, served as the first bishop of the Western Missouri Diocese of the Episcopal Church.

Her marriage to Charles Nearing ended in 1915 with his death. A few months later she accepted the matron's position. This was her first, last, and only employment.

Many thousands sought and welcomed her motherly advice and aid in solving a myriad of difficulties. There were scores of lost children, as well as elderly, foreign, disabled, sick, and newlywed travelers. "The first thing I learned about my job," Nearing said, "was that there wasn't anything routine about my routine." Her office was near the women's restroom.

June 17, 1933 was a day she never forgot: the day of the Union Station Massacre. Gangster Charles "Pretty Boy" Floyd and Adam Richetti were hired to free Frank Nash, a federal prisoner who was being transported to Leavenworth Penitentiary, as he was moved through Union Station. During their unsuccessful attempt, Nash, two Kansas City policmen, a chief of police from Oklahoma, and an FBI agent were killed in a hail of machine-gun bullets.

After more than 21 years of service at Union Station, Nearing retired in 1937. It is thought she was the first woman in the country to receive a railroad retirement pension.

From her apartment at 22 East Thirty-second Terrace, she mused, "You know, I've been so busy looking after travelers that I haven't had much time to travel myself. Maybe I'll be off soon to visit my own relatives scattered all the way from Chicago to California."

COURTESY MISSOURI VALLEY SPECIAL COLLECTIONS, KANSAS CITY PUBLIC LIBRARY, KANSAS CITY, MISSOURI

*Anna M. Nearing*

# ALICE NIELSEN

HER OPERATIC CAREER was enviable: Victor Herbert wrote light operas just for her and she sang with Enrico Caruso. She was a prima donna who remained a joyous, unaffected Kansas City girl her entire life.

Alice Nielsen was born in 1876 in Nashville, Tennessee, one of eight children of Erasmus Ivarius and Sarah Nielsen. After her father's death when she was seven years old, the family moved to Kansas City. Alice Nielsen was an exuberant, musically gifted child. A member of St. Patrick's Church choir at 800 Cherry Street, she attended St. Teresa's Academy and studied music with Max Decsi, a leading vocal coach.

Her stage debut in the starring role of *Chanticleer,* a locally written opera, was in 1892. Nielsen joined the Chicago Church Choir Company which took her to California, and she joined a comic opera group in Oakland. That failed, and she went to San Francisco's Tivoli Theater where comic opera was well established. Nielsen came into her own. In two and one-half years she sang over 150 roles including many grand opera parts appropriate for a coloratura.

Nielsen boldly auditioned for the Bostonians, the nation's most notable light opera company, won a spot, and within a year was its leading soprano. Considered an artist of uncommon ability, the top composers wrote roles for her. Victor Herbert wrote a part for Nielsen in *The Serenade,* which was such a hit that he followed it with *The Fortune Teller* and *The Singing Girl* in 1898. Her greatest fame came during these years with light opera.

In 1902 she decided to study grand opera in Italy. After two years, she made a successful debut in Naples playing Marguerite in *Faust.* The following year she played Mimi in *La Boheme* with Enrico Caruso in London. Nielsen performed with the San Carlo Opera Company, Boston Opera Company, and New York Metropolitan Opera. Though it was her goal, Nielsen never became a regular at the Met because the competition for a spot was so intense. She returned to light opera, and when the public lost interest in it, she retired.

*Alice Nielsen as she appeared in 1898 for her role in* The Fortune Teller.

Nielsen was married three times, first to Kansas Citian Benjamin Nentwig when she was quite young. All three ended in divorce.

She always considered Kansas City her home and, in fact, made her last performance here in November 1923 when she came to honor Sir Carl Busch. She donated her collection of costumes from light opera, musical scores, and other mementos of a remarkable career to the Kansas City Museum.

Alice Nielsen died on March 9, 1943, at her New York apartment where she had lived modestly for over 20 years.

# DOROTHY BURROWS PERKINS

THEY KNOW MORE about 'Perky' in London, Paris, and New York than they do in Kansas City. I doubt that for teaching ballet students there is anyone superior." Rosella Hightower, one of the principal ballerinas of the Ballet Russe de Monte Carlo and the Marquis de Cuevas Ballet, was referring to her beloved Kansas City teacher, Dorothy Burrows Perkins.

She was born in Kansas City on February 25, 1884. When she was very young, her father taught her to dance, but her mother would not allow her to perform. By the age of 18 she was instructing a

COURTESY © THE KANSAS CITY STAR COMPANY

*Dorothy Burrows Perkins*

dance class for neighborhood children, but teaching was not her goal. Burrows truly wanted to be a professional dancer, but a fall on ice in 1914 resulted in a serious back injury that ruled out strenuous exercise and thus, a career as a dancer. The accident and a divorce from Frederick G. Perkins left her financial future bleak. At the insistence of Clara Kellogg and Katherine Baxter, publishers of *The Independent*, Dorothy Perkins began teaching dance as a profession.

She instituted a program of learning and teaching, followed by more learning and teaching. Attending classes in New York City and Paris in the summer and teaching in Kansas City in the winter made up her year. She recalled asking "more questions about movement than any human being ever born, and I never taught anything I didn't know." Eventually Perkins felt she mastered how to teach dancing.

Exercise was the backbone of her method of teaching. "You start on the floor, and when you learn how to breathe, you sit up to get balance from the pelvis to the neck. Then you get on all fours and go up and down and sideways." And finally in the Perkins method a dancer got to her feet to achieve balance.

Perkins maintained that it was her exercise program that transformed Rosella Hightower, an ugly duckling with weak arches, into one of the greatest ballerinas of her time. Another famous pupil was Ula Sharon, who attained stardom in New York and appeared in a command performance for the king and queen of England. And there were hundreds of other pupils. At one point there were more than 200 of her students working in ballet or other areas of dance.

The Dorothy Perkins Studio had several locations during its existence and ended up in her home at 3921 Wyandotte Street after she sustained broken hips and a sprained back. In 1941 Perkins was named head of the dance department at the Conservatory of Music.

Dorothy Burrows Perkins died in 1981 at the age of 97. She was buried in Mount Washington Cemetery.

# NELLE NICHOLS PETERS

THE NEARLY 1,000 buildings attributed to her during her 60-year career have left an indelible mark on Kansas City's architectural heritage.

Nelle Elizabeth Nichols was born on December 11, 1884, in a sod house in Niagara, North Dakota. Around 1900 she attended Buena Vista College in Storm Lake, Iowa. She reveled in mathematics, often checking out geometry and algebra books from the library, while spending her spare time sketching and drawing. After graduation, one of her sisters suggested working in an architect's office since that would combine her bent for mathematics with her skill in art. Rejected by several firms, she was hired in 1903 by Eisentraut, Colby and Pottenger, an architectural firm in Sioux City, for $3 a week as a draftslady. She took correspondence courses in architecture.

Following a four-year apprenticeship, Nichols was transferred to the firm's Kansas City office in 1909. The lack of work prompted her to open her own business. She did all types of architectural work: residences (a $15 charge for a small home design), office buildings, and her specialty, apartments and hotels. In 1911 she married William H. Peters, a designer for the Kansas City Terminal Railroad.

In 1913 she formed an association with the Phillips Building Company, owned by Charles E. Phillips, a local developer.

*Nelle Nichols Peters*

COURTESY JACKSON COUNTY HISTORICAL SOCIETY ARCHIVES

Peters designed dozens of apartments for him including the literary group: the Robert Louis Stevenson, Eugene Field, Mark Twain, Washington Irving, Thomas Carlyle, James Russell Lowell, and the Robert Browning, all located on the west side of the Country Club Plaza.

The years following a divorce from Peters in 1923 were her most productive. Apartments, constructed around the concept of a courtyard, became her trademark. In 1924 alone she was responsible for 29 projects, including the Ambassador Hotel at 3560 Broadway, which at the time was the largest apartment-hotel in the city, and the Luzier Cosmetics Building at 3216 Gillham Plaza.

The Depression of the 1930s, followed by World War II, brought an end to the building boom and to her career as well. Her last known architectural commission was in 1956, and she officially retired in 1967. An accomplished seamstress, she made her own clothes and sewed for others as a means of supplementing her income.

Nelle Elizabeth Nichols Peters died on October 7, 1974, at the age of 90 as one of Kansas City's most prolific and least recognized architects.

# MAE REED PORTER

HER LOVE OF HISTORY began during her childhood in Glasgow, Missouri. As she watched the Missouri River from the porch of her home, her imagination was fired with thoughts of paddlewheels, the expedition of Lewis and Clark, and the American West.

Born in Dallas in 1888, she attended Iowa State College where she met and married Clyde Henderson Porter in 1910. After a try at farming in Idaho, her husband served as an ambulance driver in World War I, subsequently moving to Kansas City where he joined his father at the Kansas City Power and Light Company.

Mae Reed Porter came to be known as a serious collector of American Indian relics as well as an author, lecturer, and world traveler. In 1937 she and her daughter Jean visited the Peale Museum in Baltimore to study Lewis and Clark. They discovered a treasure trove: a collection of sketches by Alfred Jacob Miller. During 1837 and 1838, Miller had accompanied Sir William Drummond Stewart of Scotland on a hunting trip in the American West as an artist to record Indians. Miller produced about 300 sketches, over 100 of which were found in a pasteboard box stored for over a century in the museum's attic. Porter was captivated by the collection and agreed to pay $800 for it (the value was $150,000 in 1960). Returning to Kansas City, she showed the art to Paul Gardner, director of the Nelson Gallery of Art, who realized their importance and put them on display.

Porter researched the sketches thoroughly. The material she gathered resulted in a slide show and lecture entitled "The West That Was" and the first draft of a book. The January 1944 issue of *Fortune* magazine printed a separate portfolio of ten color sketches from her collection. Shortly thereafter Porter met eminent historian Bernard DeVoto. He took her 1941 draft for a book, selected the sketches, and authored *Across the Wide Missouri*, for which Porter wrote the foreword. In 1948 DeVoto received the Pulitzer Prize for history for the book. Metro-Goldwyn-Mayer premiered the movie version of the book starring Clark Gable in Kansas City at the Loew's Midland Theater in 1951.

Though history was her special interest, Porter was active in community activities including the George H. Nettleton Home for Women, Friends of Art of the Nelson Gallery, Daughters of the American Revolution, Girl Scouts Council of Greater Kansas City, Kansas City Browning Society, National League of American Penwomen, and American

*Mae Reed Porter*

Association of University Women.

In 1940 she and her husband backed the founding of a museum at the R.A. Long mansion, Corinthian Hall, at 3218 Gladstone Boulevard. The Kansas City Museum became a reality. She served it as a member of the board of governors and trustees. In 1958 she funded the Mae Reed Porter Indian room.

Mae Reed Porter died on October 23, 1968, in Santa Fe where she had moved to be near her daughter. She is remembered as a woman with a passion for the history of the early American West, the author of six books, and donor of art and artifacts to the Kansas City Museum.

# MINNA KENNEDY POWELL

FOR 22 YEARS the public knew the art and music critic of *The Kansas City Star* by the initials that ran at the bottom of the Sunday column entitled "Music and Musicians"—M.K.P. The initials stood for Minna Kennedy Powell.

Born on April 6, 1877, in a farmhouse near Red Wing, Minnesota, she was one of six children of John and Isabella Bailey. Minna attended the rural district elementary school and did daily farm chores. When she was 16 years old, her family moved across the state to a stock farm near Granite Falls where she attended high school.

She entered Carleton College to study art and music, intending to become an artist. She graduated and found a job in an engraving shop.

While on vacation she witnessed a fire that took the lives of two women at a resort. Minna Bailey called the *St. Paul Pioneer Press and Dispatch* with a telephone account of the tragedy and agreed to write the story. It was done well, and she was asked to join the paper as a reporter and music critic. In a short time she married George E. Powell, a newspaperman.

Minna K. Powell joined the staff of *The Kansas City Star* on December 6, 1915, as the music and art critic, succeeding Karl Walter, a British journalist who had left to join the British army. As a critic she was understanding, kind, and discriminating. Unless she saw some reason to question an artist's sincerity and honesty, she was not inclined to be very critical but preferred to dwell on the positive aspects of a piece of art or a performance.

She had an abiding interest in the Nelson Gallery of Art—Atkins Museum and the Kansas City Philharmonic. She was lavish in her praise for both.

Fostering the arts in Kansas City was also conducted on a personal level. Powell became interested in Marian Talley, a 14-year-old Kansas City singer. Talley's voice so astonished her that she became one of the principal organizers of a fund-raising concert that netted $10,000 for the girl's education. Five years later Talley made her singing debut at the Metropolitan Opera House in New York City.

Afflicted with a thyroid ailment that confined her to her bed, Powell reflected, "I feel I've done about all I want to do in this world, but still I'd like to live—it's fun to live!" She died on March 7, 1938, ending a 22-year career with *The Star*. Following a funeral service at Grace and Holy Trinity Cathedral at which Edna Scotten Billings played the organ, Powell was buried in St. Paul, Minnesota.

COURTESY © THE KANSAS CITY STAR COMPANY

*Minna Kennedy Powell*

# SALLY RAND
## *Helen Gould Beck*

I WANT TO LIVE to be 117, have a glass of pink champagne, dance the Vienna waltz with a nice man, and sleep late the next morning. After that I don't give a damn." Sally Rand fell a bit short of her goal when she died at the age of 75.

Helen Gould Beck, a girl who literally fanned her way to fame and fortune, considered Kansas City her hometown. She was born April 3, 1904, in Hickory County, Missouri, the daughter of William F. and Annette Beck. After their parents separated, Billie, as she was called then, her brother, and mother moved to Kansas City. Living at 2904 Forest Avenue, she attended Greenwood School. When just six years old, she watched Anna Pavlova, the famous Russian ballerina, perform and was so moved that she vowed to become a ballerina and began taking dancing lessons. After graduating from Central High School in 1921, she spent a year at Christian College (now Columbia College) in Columbia, Missouri. College life was not for Billie Beck.

Show business beckoned. Billie Beck appeared in several local fashion shows and amateur theatricals, finally hitting the road with Gus Edwards, a well-known vaudeville star. While on tour, she suffered an attack of appendicitis in Hollywood. During her recovery she attracted the attention of Mack Sennett, who cast her in her first movie.

*Sally Rand in souvenir program, Class of 1915-16, Auditorium Theatre, July 6, 1919.*

COURTESY MISS SUSANNAH GENTRY

She made a big splash, literally, when her role called for diving 35 feet into a tank of water.

But, in 1926 her career was launched when she became the leading lady of the Cecile B. DeMille Players with the new name of Sally Rand (DeMille insisted on the change). In signing her, he observed that "her piquancy, coupled with a rare beauty of face and form and her ability as an actress are bound to make her a tremendous screen personality." Sally Rand acted in DeMille's 1926 production of *The Last Frontier* and had several other screen credits, but by the end of the twenties she was a has-been at the tender age of 26. Talkies were in and Rand was out.

With a career switch, she became a part of show business history. At the 1933 Chicago World's Fair she electrified audiences with a fan dance to the music of Claude Debussy's "Clair de Lune." With dimmed lights, soft music, a flesh-colored body suit, and two constantly moving fans, Rand was by far the most popular attraction on the midway. Giving the illusion of nudity got her arrested four times

COURTESY MISSOURI VALLEY SPECIAL COLLECTIONS, KANSAS CITY PUBLIC LIBRARY, KANSAS CITY, MISSOURI

*Sally Rand in a bubble, wearing a flesh-colored body suit.*

for indecent exposure on the *first* day of the fair. "It was terribly humiliating. My God, I'd never had even a traffic ticket in my life!" During her career, the queen of the fan dancers (by the way, she copyrighted the dance) frequently substituted bubbles for the fans.

She was a big star for several decades but failed at marriage three times because her career took precedence over home life. She often visited Kansas City, performing at the Tower Theater, 213 East Twelfth Street, and the Folly Theater. In 1972 at the age of 68 she danced at the Bacchus Ball held in Union Station. Rand donated a number of her personal effects to a benefit auction for the Folly Theater in 1976 and once again glided across the stage in her flesh-

*Sally Rand arriving in Kansas City around 1950.*

colored tights, carrying two large fans. Her last visit was a benefit for Historic Kansas City Foundation in 1978.

A rigid exercise schedule kept her 5'1" frame in fine shape. "If you love living, you try to take care of the equipment." When asked if she had any plans to retire, she replied, "When they screw the top down on the coffin, or when I break a leg."

Sally Rand died August 31, 1979, in Glendora, California, of congestive heart failure.

# NELL DONNELLY REED

H ER DISTASTE FOR frumpy, shapeless, 69-cent housedresses led to the creation of a stylish, feminine frock which was the foundation of a multi-million dollar business.

Ellen Quinlan was born March 6, 1889, in Parsons, Kansas. Her father had immigrated from County Cork, Ireland, to work on the railroad. Ellen, or Nell as she was called, was the twelfth of 13 children and received her early education at a local Catholic convent. After high school graduation she married Paul J. Donnelly, credit manager for Barton Shoe Company, and moved with him to Kansas City.

COURTESY © THE KANSAS CITY STAR COMPANY

*Nell Donnelly Reed*

In 1916 women, who usually did not work outside the home, tended to wear housedresses. Functional yes, stylish no. Since Nell Donnelly was concerned with *her* appearance, she stitched up a new style of dress. Wearing her smart, colorful housedress, she was immediately besieged with offers from neighbors to buy dresses.

At first she personally attempted to fill all requests but soon had to employ two women. Sensing that she might well have an item that could take off in sales, she took a sample to the George B. Peck Dry Goods Company and left the store with an order for 18-dozen dresses to be delivered in two months. With less than $1,500 Nell Donnelly opened a small factory downtown and filled the order on time. The retail price per dress was an unheard of $1, but women flocked to the stores for her product.

With the help of her husband who had returned from World War I, the Donnelly Garment Company was established in 1919. Paul Donnelly served as president and Nell as secretary. But, she had her hand in every phase of the business. She studied the market to learn who wore her dresses when and where, oversaw the careful testing of fabrics, and went to Paris for design inspiration. Nell Donnelly strove to please her customers with varied styles at affordable prices.

By 1931 the Donnelly Garment Company had enjoyed tremendous growth; it had 1,000 employees and sales of $3.5 million. But there was a dark side to this success.

On December 16, 1931, Nell and her chauffeur were pulling into the driveway of her home at 5255 Oak Street around 6 P.M. when three men seized them. They were held hostage in Bonner Springs, Kansas, with the kidnappers demanding a ransom payment of $75,000 and threatening to blind Nell. No money was paid, but the two were released unharmed after a day and one-half of terror because of the efforts of Senator James A. Reed, an old family friend. Shortly after her release she obtained a divorce from Donnelly and in 1933 married Reed, a former mayor of Kansas City and a three-term United States senator.

Nell Donnelly Reed was first and foremost an astute businesswoman. With her as executive director, the company survived depressions, recessions, wars abroad, and battles at home with the federal government over regulations. She was a leader in bringing about better working conditions. Hers was the first Kansas City company to pay for group hospitalization, provide welfare benefits, and make educational opportunities available for workers and their children. Because they were satisfied, her workers voted not to join a union (it wasn't until 1968 that they were unionized). She sold her interest in the company in 1956.

NBC Radio presented her story in "The Golden Needle," starring Dorothy McGuire as Nell, in 1950.

There was another side of Nell Reed, that of contributor to Kansas City. She was active in the Women's Chamber of Commerce and served on the boards of Lindenwood College, Kansas City Art Institute, Starlight Theater Association, and the Kansas City Board of Education. She was listed in *Who's Who of American Women* in 1951. That same year she became the first woman elected to the board of trustees of Midwest Research Institute.

Nell Donnelly Reed, the grand lady of the garment industry, died September 8, 1991, at the age of 102.

# KATHERINE BERRY RICHARDSON

W HEN SHE DIED, she was described as the most important woman in Kansas City. Katherine Berry Richardson had devoted her life to the needs of the community and sacrificed financial reward so that Children's Mercy Hospital might flourish.

Katherine Berry was born around 1860 (she never revealed the exact date) in Cave Springs, Kentucky, the younger of two daughters of Stephen and Harriet Berry. Her father, a Union sympathizer, was forced to flee for

*Dr. Katherine Berry Richardson*

his life during the Civil War, leaving behind his wife and daughters. Returning at the end of the war, he found himself a widower and his mill business in ruins. He and his two daughters, Katherine and Alice, moved to Pennsylvania where they were reared according to his creed: "Wherever you go, it is your duty to make good citizens of your neighbors." It was a lesson they never forgot.

The sisters chose careers in dentistry and medicine, most unusual professions for women of their day. Alice taught school so that Katherine could attend Pennsylvania Women's Medical College. Then Katherine helped her sister study for a degree in dentistry. A flip of a coin determined that she would practice medicine in LaCrosse, Wisconsin. During their first and only separation the sisters both married; Alice Graham's husband died, and James Ira Richardson, whom Katherine married in 1893, died in 1908. Alice joined her sister in the mid-1890s, and they came to Kansas City.

For a while they lived and practiced in the Ridge Building. They later moved into a large house at 121 Clinton Place. The sisters worked in the face of bigotry and prejudice, to which Richardson exhibited a fierce impatience that was to mark her entire career.

COURTESY MISSOURI VALLEY SPECIAL COLLECTIONS, KANSAS CITY PUBLIC LIBRARY, KANSAS CITY, MISSOURI

*Dr. Alice Berry Graham*

Mercy Hospital had its beginning the night of June 1, 1897, when Alice Berry Graham rescued a five-year-old crippled, emaciated girl from her mother who had been attempting to give the child away at saloons. Appalled by this situation, the sisters took the child to a maternity hospital run by Dr. Avis E. Smith and rented a bed. From then on Richardson and Graham devoted their lives to the cause of mercy for children.

Shortly afterward the hospital was abandoned by the organization running it, and Drs. Graham and Richardson were given the two-year lease on the building and $13 worth of old furniture. Mercy

Hospital for crippled children was opened on June 11, 1897. No sick or crippled child was ever turned away because of an inability to pay for treatment. Their dream became reality when a new hospital building went up on Independence Avenue in 1916, but Alice Graham did not live to see it. Although her sister had died in 1913, Richardson gave her credit as the founder of Mercy Hospital. However, it was Richardson who made it work. She organized, administrated, solicited funds, and treated patients. With red hair and a fiery temper, she drove her colleagues as hard as she drove herself but formed a talented, unpaid staff of physicians and surgeons. She did earn a meager living from an outside practice but could never be persuaded to accept one penny for her service to Mercy.

Katherine Richardson established a Mercy Hospital ward at Wheatley Hospital where white nurses worked with black nurses in training. For her surgical skills she was elected to the American College of Physicians and Surgeons. She sought no personal recognition and, in fact, forbade it with one exception. Two years before her death she accepted an honorary degree in law from her alma mater, Mount Union College from which she had received a bachelor's and a master's degree in philosophy. Thomas Alva Edison was honored at the same ceremony.

She was a very exceptional woman, one who preferred things plain, sturdy, and of the highest quality. Her clothes were that way, the hospital, too. She was a first-class furniture maker who produced simple, graceful furniture for all the rooms of Nurses Hall (which was a gift of Mrs. Joseph T. Bird and her daughter). Another hobby was growing flowers, shrubs, vines, and trees.

Her work came to an end on June 3, 1933. Nurses from Mercy and Wheatley hospitals stood on either side of her bier in Nurses Hall. The brief funeral service was held under her favorite tree on the grounds of the hospital.

Though rich in accomplishments, she left an estate valued at less than $3,500. What she did amass was a lifetime of working to make her neighbors better citizens. She is buried beside Alice Berry Graham in Mount Washington Cemetery.

# ANNIE RICKETTS

THEY WERE YOUNG men, many under 30 years of age and unmarried who had come to Kansas City as bankers, lawyers, physicians, newspapermen, druggists, and businessmen seeking fame and fortune. When they looked for room and board accommodations in what was already a flourishing boarding house community, there was no spot more notable or fashionable than the little yellow house located at 917 Locust Street owned and operated by Annie Ricketts.

From 1884 to 1916 "Miss Annie" or "Sis," as she was affectionately called by her boarders, provided a real home for them. She was famous for her cooking; her table was laden with delicious food served at affordable prices.

Several years before she closed the boarding house doors, Annie Ricketts' "boys" held a reunion as a gesture of thanks to her. Over 100 attended or sent words of appreciation for her motherly care.

Annie Ricketts died at her home at 4133 Locust Street of apoplexy on February 22, 1929. Her pallbearers, chosen from among her ex-boarders, included such prominent community leaders as E.A. Jaccard, Judge E.E. Porterfield, D. Austin Latchaw, and R.L. Winter. Burial was in Elmwood Cemetery.

# HAZELLE HEDGES ROLLINS

IT ALL BEGAN with the boy next door. Donald Newlin had received two poorly made Italian marionettes. He wanted more but could not find them. Twenty-two-year-old Hazelle Hedges, who lived with her parents at 815 West Fifty-ninth Street, was convinced that she could make something better . . . and she did. The word spread and from this beginning grew the only marionette factory in the United States and one of the largest in the world.

Hazelle Hedges was born January 12, 1910, the daughter of Ralph and Jessie Hazell Hedges. Her father was president of the Columbian Hog and Cattle Powder Company. Following her graduation from Westport High School, Hazelle enrolled in the School of Fine Arts at the University of Kansas and graduated in 1932. After a year at the Kansas City Art Institute, she joined the staff of the Nelson Gallery of Art—Atkins Museum making marionettes and staging plays for children. Everything came together for her: an interest in dolls and their construction, a love of children, a talent in art and design, and a flair for dramatics.

She realized the marionette market was virtually untapped since there were none produced in the United States. Before making a commitment to opening

*Hazelle Hedges Rollins*

COURTESY JOHN W. ROLLINS, JR.

a business, Hazelle Hedges spent a summer in New York City with Tony Sarg, one of the greatest marionette artists of the day. Afterwards, convinced of the market and her abilities, she opened a small factory and made her first sale to Emery, Bird, Thayer Company for the 1934 Christmas season. The next year she went to the New York Toy Fair and returned home with orders from all over the United States and many foreign countries. (Eventually the company supplied many stores, including F.A.O. Schwartz, Macy's, and the Fred Harvey Company.) Hazelle Marionettes was a going concern.

Production of the puppets was time-consuming and labor intensive. Hazelle designed her own machinery, had it made, and installed at the factory at 822 Broadway. Many features of the machinery and marionette construction were patented. The heads, hands, and often the feet were made from sawdust combined with a chemical mixture that required a month for seasoning. The parts were then suspended from a belt and dipped with 15 coats of lacquer to create a complexion. Heads were hand painted and fitted with wigs. Everything was closely scrutinized by Hazelle who gave finishing touches with her brush. When the factory moved in 1949 to a three-story converted apartment building at 905 East Tenth Street, a new method was introduced. An injection molding machine turned out tinted plastic heads at the rate of two a minute; this reduced production time by 30 days.

In 1941 Hazelle married J. Woodson Rollins, an industrial engineer, who became a partner in the company. He relieved Hazelle of the engineering, advertising, and sales end of the business.

She felt that the secret to the success of Hazelle Marionettes was that few customers were content with just one. Each year new characters were added to the line: Mother Goose characters, Space Flyer, Sweet Sue, Buckaroo Bill, Larry Long Legs, and the Blue Fairy. To help children begin to understand other nationalities and races, she introduced Señor Carlos, Rosita the Gypsy, Tony the Vendor, Indian Maiden, and others. The all-time favorite was Toto the Clown. She developed an airplane control of the strings of marionettes that was easy for children to operate.

In 1958 Hazelle, Inc. was located at 1224 Admiral Boulevard and by 1962 was the world's largest exclusive manufacturer of marionettes. In 1975, the year she retired, 250,000 were produced.

*A 1962 label for one of Hazelle Hedges Rollins' finger puppets.*

When she sold the company after 43 years of commercial puppet production, she had designed 300 puppets and held four patents.

Community activities were also of interest to Hazelle Rollins. In 1957 she was appointed a member of the Women's Kansas City Commission for International Relations and Trade by Mayor H. Roe Bartle. She served as a director of the Kansas City Women's Chamber of Commerce, the first woman to chair the Kansas City Advisory Council of the Small Business Administration, president of the Nelson Gallery Art Study Club, and president of the Republican Club for Business and Professional Women of the area in 1960. Rollins was the founder of Puppeteers of America. In 1969 she was selected as one of the three most outstanding businesswomen in Missouri by Phi Chi Theta and in 1971 as a Pen Woman of Distinction by the National League of American Pen Women.

Hazelle Hedges Rollins died March 25, 1984. Entombment was at Mount Moriah Cemetery.

# SOPHIA ROSENBERGER

SHE WAS THE epitome of everyone's favorite teacher. Sophia Rosenberger was respected and in some cases adored by her pupils.

She was born on April 30, 1866, one of six children. Her father, Gabriel Rosenberger, was a watchmaker in Davenport, Iowa. The family moved to 920 Central Street, and Sophia Rosenberger graduated from Central High School in May 1883 in a graduation ceremony held at the Coates Opera House.

Rosenberger began her teaching career at Franklin Elementary School at Fourteenth and Washington streets, just two blocks from

her home at 1229 Washington Street. In 1893 six-year-old Alexander Woollcott entered her second grade class and fell under her spell; he would remain devoted to her for the rest of his life.

Rosenberger attended Harvard University in the summer of 1898 and received a certificate for taking a course in elementary school English composition. After joining the faculty of Central High School, she went to the University of Chicago for course work in teaching high school English. She transferred to Westport

*Sophia Rosenberger in 1922.*

COURTESY MRS. DAVID J. BENJAMIN

High School and remained there for 33 years.

Rosenberger knew how to teach and she loved to teach. Her guiding principles were that reading should be a joy rather than a chore and that the reader should realize words are meant to express, not to conceal, thoughts. It was her own enthusiasm and skillful teaching technique that stimulated her pupils' interest in literature by making the classics live. As proof of how she had reached her students, her own library contained an entire shelf of books written by former pupils.

There were many well-known adults who had studied with Rosenberger: John B. Gage, mayor of Kansas City; Robert L. Mehornay, president of the Kansas City Board of Education; Morton T. Jones, president of the Chamber of Commerce; Clyde Brion Davis, author of *The Great American Novel*; Martha Scott, movie actress; and William Powell, movie actor. When asked if Powell had indeed been her pupil, she replied, "He never worked hard at being anybody's pupil."

Perhaps her most famous student was Alexander Woollcott. They enjoyed a lasting, warm friendship. In fact, she teasingly named her terrier Aleck for him. Woollcott wrote to Rosenberger in November 1942: "I stipulate if convenient, that you arrange to live until next September and I for my part will try to do the same. We must celebrate the fiftieth anniversary of my entering your class." Woollcott died six months later.

Rosenberger was active at Temple B'nai Jehudah where she served as the Sunday school principal from 1910-18. Studying Hebrew was made a part of the curriculum.

A heart condition forced her to restrict her teaching and traveling (and thus time spent with close friend Minna K. Powell). In 1940 she did agree to become a substitute teacher for an hour a day. She retired in 1943 and died on November 30, 1945. Sophia Rosenberger, teacher and inspiration, was buried at Rose Hill Cemetery.

# AGNES H. ROUSE

WARNED THAT IT WAS absolute folly for a woman to even consider this line of work, Agnes "Lena" Rouse ignored the well-intentioned advice and became the first woman to hold a seat on the Kansas City Livestock Exchange.

Born around 1873 in Aberdeen, Scotland, she was introduced early to the livestock game since her father raised and exhibited cattle. After coming to America, she saw similar sights on her brother's Kansas ranch before her marriage to John R. Rouse.

Her husband came to Kansas City in 1878 when the cattle market was rapidly expanding. His business grew, and he bought a seat on the Kansas City Livestock Exchange. Following his death in 1897, Lena Rouse was told by friends and associates that the business was no place for a woman. She decided to sell the seat on the exchange but two years later reevaluated the situation. She wanted their son, John, Jr., to have a business to enter when he grew up so she had to make a decision. "I always have been familiar with cattle and cattle terms. . . . So it was only logical that when the time came for me to consider a business for myself, I should turn to the one I knew best." She opened the A.H. Rouse Commission Company and bought a seat on the Kansas City Livestock Exchange. She was its only woman member and held the seat for about 30 years.

Lena Rouse had hopes that her son would take over the business, and he became a

*Agnes H. Rouse*

COURTESY MISSOURI VALLEY SPECIAL COLLECTIONS, KANSAS CITY PUBLIC LIBRARY, KANSAS CITY, MISSOURI

familiar figure riding a pony around the stockyards. He even began to purchase calves on his own before he died when barely a teenager. Rouse's friends assumed she would retire, but she busied herself in her work to ease the sorrow.

From her office on the fifth floor of the Livestock Exchange Building at 1600 Genessee Street, she looked down on pens packed with almost every known breed of cattle. Mondays were the biggest days with as many as 50,000 head sold. By the end of such a day millions of dollars worth of business would have been transacted. Bills were submitted to a broker, such as Rouse, for processing.

Lena Rouse was active in community organizations. She was a member of the Women's Commercial Club, Woman's City Club, and Soroptimist International of Kansas City.

Loneliness, ill health, and several years of declining business became too much of a burden to bear. On May 24, 1933, Agnes H. Rouse took her life with a self-inflicted bullet wound in her room at the Phillips Hotel and was buried at Elmwood Cemetery.

# ANNIE J. SCOTT

THERE WAS NO stopping this penniless orphan. Annie J. Scott became a teacher, missionary, author, doctor, real estate speculator, architect, builder, and contractor.

Orphaned at the age of six, she went to live with a farm family in Lafayette County, Missouri, working from dawn to dusk. By the time she was ten years old, she prepared three meals a day for a family of ten.

A visit to the farm by a woman and her two daughters changed Scott's life. She overheard them speak of the wonders of the big city of Warrensburg, Missouri, and the State Normal School there. "That talk," she said, "awoke in me the first definite determination to better my condition. I said to myself, 'This woman's girls are no smarter than I am—I, too, will attend the Warrensburg Normal School!'"

She reached an agreement with her employer allowing her to milk several cows, churn the cream, and sell the butter. In a few months Scott had saved $50. With her few possessions tied in a bundle, she rode to Warrensburg Normal School on the seat of a farm wagon. There she poured out her lifetime savings and announced that at the age of 14 she had come to enroll. Scott had to work the entire time to pay for her education, but she graduated just three years later in 1894 as a teacher.

However, she changed her mind and decided to become a Methodist home missionary. She entered the Scarritt Bible and Training School in Kansas City, again working to pay her expenses. Following graduation, Scott was appointed by the church as state secretary of the Epworth League. It was a physically demanding position. Traveling and lecturing brought on a collapse severe enough to require hospitalization. While recovering, she wrote several books of Bible stories for children . . . and decided to become a physician.

With the encouragement and support of Dr. George Halley, Scott entered the medical college of the University of Kansas in 1897. She graduated third in a large class made up almost entirely of male students. Because there was a smallpox epidemic in Kansas City, she was hired by the city and worked in the isolation ward, treating 2,500 patients. She accumulated a nest egg of $2,000 by the time she quit her job in 1902.

Dr. Halley continued to be her friend and also became her financial advisor. He suggested that she invest her money with him and E.G. Dudley in a plot of undeveloped land located between Forty-third and Forty-fifth streets on State Line Road. The plan was to make a small initial payment on the 11-acre tract, divide the land into small lots, and quickly sell them before any payments

*Dr. Annie J. Scott*

COURTESY LANDMARKS COMMISSION OF KANSAS CITY, MISSOURI

were due. It worked, yielding Scott $7,000 for the $2,000 invested. Flush with success, the three partners purchased an adjoining 20-acre tract that cleared $55,000. "From then on I became a speculator in real estate as a business," Scott recalled.

She saw the potential profitability in constructing and selling homes so she struck out on her own as a home builder. Between 1904 and 1909 she oversaw the building and marketing of over 200 houses which cleared more than $100,000 for her. This was an amazing achievement for a young woman of 33, who had been a poor, uneducated orphan living on a farm.

Because of her childhood, she abhorred wasting time, money, and materials. She held construction costs to a minimum by serving as architect, personally buying the required materials, opening a stone quarry that supplied rock needed for the foundations, and overseeing each job. Scott was the boss. Her weekly payroll varied between $1,000 and $2,000, and she made sure every dollar of it was earned.

Once again overwork and stress affected her health. Ordered by her doctor to stop working, she went to Mexico for relaxation, leaving behind a number of uncompleted projects. Since no one ran the business for her, problems grew and lawsuits were filed. Fortunately, she was able to return in time to salvage a part of her investment.

Despite building houses for others, Scott chose to live at the Densmore Hotel for a number of years. She married Dr. Maxwell Branner, a New York City surgeon who served in World War I. After the war, he lived in Kansas City for a short time before leaving to publish a medical journal in the East. Scott remained in Kansas City.

Hailed as the city's foremost self-made woman, Scott replied, "I never have doubted my ability to succeed. I simply would not contemplate the possibility of failure."

# RUTH NORDBERG SEUFERT

W HAT DOES IT TAKE to become a famous impresario? Many would say a strong personality and a sturdy constitution, and more of both if you're a woman. Ruth Nordberg Seufert was such a woman and for almost 40 years exerted a profound influence on the cultural life of the community.

Ruth Nordberg was born July 5, 1897, in Bonner Springs, Kansas, to a musical family. Her father, Olaf G. Nordberg, a native of Sweden, was a musician who played the violin and cello, and two of her brothers played in the old Nighthawks radio orchestra on WDAF. Ruth trained as a pianist and, while attending Northeast High School, gave lessons for 25 cents an hour.

Olaf Nordberg's home at 615 Spruce Avenue was always open to fellow Swedes. One who received the family's hospitality was Arno Seufert, a young musician who had studied at the Royal Academy of Stockholm and was a graduate of the University of Upsala. Six years later, in 1918, Ruth and Arno were married. Her husband,

*Ruth Nordberg Seufert*

a cellist with the Kansas City Philharmonic for many years, died in 1954.

Ruth Seufert's entrance into the local professional music world came in the early 1930s with selling subscriptions to Philharmonic concerts. And sell she could. In 1941 she was appointed its business manager with the formidable task of solving its financial problems. But late 1941 brought

America's entry into World War II, and support for cultural arts in Kansas City diminished. However, her sales ability was so amazing that when she resigned five years later, the books showed an $8,000 surplus.

Her independence and entrepreneurship resulted in the opening of Ruth Seufert Celebrity Attractions which brought famous singers, pianists, musicians, and performers to Kansas City. Her first season opened in 1946 with the appearance of Eleanor Steber, renowned soprano with the Metropolitan Opera Company. Over the years she booked a panoply of international stars, including Leontyne Price, Anna Moffo, Marcel Marceau, Van Cliburn, Vladimir Horowitz, and the Bolshoi Theater. Variety and high quality were her goals. She said, "Kansas City has a wonderful musical audience. People come expecting to hear a first-class performance and are knowledgeable enough to know when they are getting it."

There was another side to Seufert, that of master chef. She had learned her mother's culinary secrets, inherited her father's hospitable nature, and loved to prepare meals for her famous and not-so-famous friends.

Seufert was a member of the Woman's City Club, Women's Chamber of Commerce, Kansas City Business and Professional Women's Club, International Association of Concert and Festival Managers, and Order of the Eastern Star. In 1972 she received the distinguished service to music award from the Kansas City Musical Club.

Ruth Nordberg Seufert died January 25, 1975, and was buried in Mount Moriah Cemetery. John Haskins, music editor of *The Kansas City Star*, wrote, "I would like to think you might yet assemble a choir of angels and book them into the Music Hall, and I'd be there in the same aisle seat, counting the house, and congratulating you on your good taste."

# MATHILDE DALLMEYER SHELDEN

I T WAS WHEN ten-year-old Dolly Dallmeyer demanded to know why she could not vote that she actually embarked on her career of championing women's rights.

Dolly was born December 6, 1885, one of five children of Rudolph and Louise Schmidt Dallmeyer. Her father immigrated from Germany and in 1871 settled in Jefferson City where he was the leading dry goods merchant in the area. Her maternal grandfather served as the mayor of the town. Following graduation from Jefferson City High School, Dallmeyer attended National Park Seminary in Washington, D.C., where she was introduced to civic, club, and political opportunities available to women. After her return to Jefferson City, she joined several local women's clubs and began assuming a role as leader in community affairs and champion of women's rights.

*Mathilde (Dolly) Dallmeyer Shelden*

Dallmeyer, a pioneer in the Missouri suffrage movement, organized the Jefferson City Equal Suffrage League. She scheduled a series of campaign speeches covering 21 Missouri counties which sometimes necessitated an overnight stay. So controversial was the prospect of women voting that several times she and her chaperone were refused accommodations. A versatile, witty, and magnetic speaker, she held audiences spellbound.

She was a Republican even though her father had been an ardent

Democrat. "It took," she said, "all of my convictions to publicly announce my political position in Jefferson City, a Democratic stronghold. I made my choice for the Republican Party as it more nearly approached my concept of the science of government." After women received the right to vote, Dolly transferred her energy to working for the Republican Party.

In 1919 she was elected vice-president of the Missouri State Republican Club and

**Women Suffrage Meeting**

at the Court house

**Saturday, Feb. 15th**

at 2:30 p. m.

MRS. DAN W. KNEFLER of St. Louis, of State Propaganda Committee, will speak, also

MISS MATHILDE K. DALLMEYER Vice-President of Jefferson City Equal Suffrage League, and

MRS. J. F. WALKER will talk.

**Everybody Invited**

COURTESY DR RUSSELL D. SHELDEN

became the first woman to hold political office in the state. That same year she was a delegate to the first national conference of Republicans in Washington, D.C. The following year she became a member of the first state committee to which women were elected. She also married Frank Elwin Shelden, a prominent orthodontist, and came as a bride to 1272 West Fifty-ninth Street, her home for many years.

Marriage did not diminish her involvement in the community. In 1924, she was appointed a member of the upper house of the City Council, filling a vacancy created by the death of Emma Lard Longan. She served in this post for two years. About the same time she became a member of the Twentieth Century Club, the official Republican organization for women in Kansas City. Several years later she was elected its president.

There were a number of other interests for Dolly Shelden. Gardening was important to her, and she was president of the Kansas City Rose Society as well as the Browning Society and Kansas City Dental Society Auxiliary. Additionally she was active at the Kansas City Art Institute, Friends of Art, Women's Philharmonic, Lyric Theater, Kansas City Museum, Girl Scouts Council of Greater Kansas City, and YWCA. She was a member of the Kansas City Athenaeum, Women's City Club, and Kansas City Musical Club.

Dolly Shelden died January 17, 1980, and will be remembered and appreciated for her role in serving as an advocate for women's rights.

# VIVIAN DAVIS SHEPHERD

WHEN SHE LEARNED from a report by the Kansas City Council of Social Agencies there were 350 disabled persons in the area who could not qualify for assistance from any agency but who could become self-supporting to varying degrees with the right help, Vivian Davis Shepherd went to work.

A graduate of Central Missouri State College and the holder of a master's degree in counseling from the University of Missouri-Kansas City, Shepherd taught elementary school in northern Missouri for three years, followed by five years in office management and public relations with Postal Telegraph. She married James R. Shepherd, a teacher in Kansas City, and had a daughter.

Because she wanted to serve others more directly, she became the assistant to the supervisor of the local Missouri state vocational rehabilitation office in 1942. She suggested that the rehabilitation needs and services available in the area be evaluated. In 1946 the Kansas City Council of Social Agencies announced the findings which prompted an outcry for reform of the system. The next year the Rehabilitation Institute was formed with the purpose of providing physical therapy, prevocational training, and placement for the severely disabled in the region. Those affected by disease, accident, or birth disabilities were eligible for the services. With the aid and support of Mrs. Eleanor Jones Kemper, the institute opened with 30 worker-patients, $7,500 in the bank, a budget of $30,000, and Vivian Shepherd as executive director.

*Vivian Davis Shepherd*

COURTESY REHABILITATION INSTITUTE

She was given a year's leave of absence from her state job. That year extended to 27.

The institute opened in 1947 on the second floor of a remodeled building at 2700 McGee Street Trafficway. The patient load continued to increase. With the financial assistance of Clara Lewis Stover, facilities were moved in 1950 to a two-story building at 3600 Troost Avenue, the former location of Monkey Cleaners and Dyers. By 1968 the number of patients had doubled, and larger quarters were again needed. The following year the institute occupied its first permanent home at 3011 Baltimore Avenue. Built at a cost of $3 million, it became one of the nation's most complete rehabilitation centers under one roof. Regarded as a model in the field, professionals came from all parts of the world to study.

Because of her competence, compassion, and professional skills, Shepherd received national and international recognition. She served as president of the National Rehabilitation Association and the National Association of Sheltered Workshops and Homebound Programs. Also, she was vice-president of the Association of Rehabilitation Centers, chairman of the National Institute on Workshop Standards, and a member of the board of the Metropolitan Council on Developmental Disabilities.

Shepherd had many interests outside her professional world as a member of the Friends of Art of Nelson Gallery, Historic Kansas City Foundation, Truman Library Institute, Kansas City Ballet Association, Rose Brooks Center, and the International Relations Council as well as a board member of the Women's Chamber of Commerce. She served as a volunteer at the Shepherd's Center for 15 years. In 1959 and 1982 she received the distinguished alumni award from the University of Missouri-Kansas City.

Vivian Davis Shepherd, a founder of the Rehabilitation Institute, retired in 1974 and died at the age of 87 on April 8, 1992.

# AVIS E. SMITH

D R. AVIS E. SMITH closed a distinguished medical career at the age of 80 with the satisfaction of just having delivered a set of twins. She was the first female physician qualified to practice in Jackson County.

Born in Rockford, Illinois, on October 17, 1851, she entered medicine, a profession that ostracized women. Smith enrolled at the University of Illinois just four years after its founding and after graduation taught for three years before entering the Women's Medical College in Chicago in 1877. She was accepted for an internship by the New England Hospital for Women and Children in Boston where only female doctors and nurses were permitted to work.

While a student at the University of Illinois, Smith had become friends with Mr. and Mrs. Henry M. Beardsley, who lived in Kansas City. Learning that Smith had completed her internship, they invited her to come visit, hoping that she could be persuaded to stay and open a practice. Smith came but had no intention of remaining in Kansas City primarily because of her distaste for lawlessness which was epitomized by the activities of the Jesse James gang. However, fate intervened. While still visiting, Smith, who was trained in obstetrics, was consulted about a woman who had had a complicated pregnancy and was soon to deliver. The mother-to-be was a member of the James family, but Smith said later, "I had no choice but to take the case." Dr. Smith stayed here and became the James family physician.

Her specialty was obstetrics and gynecology. In the early 1880s Drs. Smith and Martha Cleveland Dibble shared an office at 309 Commerce Building. They were later joined in their practice by Dr. Eliza Mitchell and moved to the G.Y. Smith Building on the northwest corner of Eleventh and Main streets.

Knowing that many women preferred a female physician, they decided to open their own hospital, the Women's and Children's Hospital. It began in 1897 in a small house at Fifteenth Street and Cleveland Avenue, but soon larger quarters were needed. In 1899 they moved into a building at Eleventh Street and Troost Avenue.

By this time they had accumulated about $2,000 which allowed setting up two free beds for those who could not afford to pay. Smith was elected president of the board of directors. By 1902 under her leadership the treasury had grown to over $15,000. The medical staff included Drs. Annette Peet, L.G. Rummel, Alice Graham (a dentist in charge of free beds), Katherine B. Richardson (head of surgery), and Emily Colt (head of internal medicine). Out of this hospital grew Children's Mercy Hospital because of the vision and dedication of Graham and Richardson.

Smith became a familiar sight in town. She preferred to walk or ride her bicycle on house calls, even though many were at night. She was an active member of the Kansas City Athenaeum and the New England Women's Club.

Avis E. Smith, one of the women who so capably carried the medical banner from the 1880s into the 1930s, died at her home, 3119 Olive Street, on January 10, 1941 and was buried in Elmwood Cemetery. A most fitting tribute to her were the 20 children named in her honor.

# LAURA CONYERS SMITH

A WOMAN WHO LOVED roses made her dream of a municipal rose garden come true in Loose Park.

Laura Conyers was born about 1882 in St. Helens, Oregon. Before coming to Kansas City in 1912, she and her sister married brothers: Mary became the wife of Ernest E. Smith and Laura of Clifford Bradley Smith.

Although Laura and Mary Smith admired the beautiful homes and trees of Kansas City, they missed seeing roses that

*Laura Conyers Smith*

grew so profusely in Oregon. Local nurserymen and gardeners told them emphatically that roses were not suited to Kansas City's growing conditions, but the Smiths refused to believe such advice. The sisters built a rose garden of more than 500 bushes at Mary's home at 814 Westover Road. In 1929 Mary and Ernest Smith died unexpectedly, and Laura and Clifford Smith inherited the home and garden.

The concept of a rose garden for public enjoyment blossomed during the dark days of the Depression. Smith invited a few of her friends to her house to listen to an NBC Radio program sponsored by the American Rose Society. This led to the organization of the Kansas City branch of the American Rose Society on May 9, 1931, in Smith's living room.

A month later the 135-member club held its first rose show in that same living room. Over 1,000 people attended. With such a show of public enthusiasm, Smith began to consider a municipal rose garden. She approached the Kansas City Parks Department. The idea was well received, and Smith was appointed to the original committee that met with the parks board to determine a site.

The garden, which the parks department agreed to construct and maintain, began in Loose Park with 16 small rose beds displaying 120 rose bushes. Laura and Clifford Smith and her brother donated the first pergola in the garden, and the Kansas City Rose Society furnished the plants. The circular layout with a reflecting pool and fountain was designed by S. Herbert Hare, a landscape architect. In 1965 the garden was officially renamed the Laura Conyers Smith Municipal Rose Garden.

Laura Smith received many accolades for her accomplishments. In 1954 she was honored by Theta Sigma Phi for distinguished service in the fields of horticulture and community service. Smith served as the president of the Kansas City Rose Society for 11 years and was financial secretary and treasurer of the Amateur Flower Gardeners Association. She was a member of the Kansas City Music Club and the women's division of the Kansas City Museum.

Though Laura Conyers Smith died January 28, 1968, her garden lives on as testimony to the woman who loved roses and wanted to share that love with the community.

# LENA RIVERS SMITH

S HE HAD INTELLIGENCE and poise and, seemingly, enjoyed success as a black newswoman on television. But only her close friends were aware of all the slights and rejections that Lena Rivers Smith had endured to get to where she was.

Born on March 15, 1922, in Kansas City, she was one of seven children of Isaac and Evadene Smith. She attended Wendell Phillips School and Lincoln High School and in 1943 graduated from Lincoln University. A few years later Smith did graduate work at Northwestern University. Returning to Kansas City, she went to work for *The Call* and remained there from 1950 until early 1965. During those 15 years at the newspaper Smith held the positions of society editor, crime reporter, and city editor.

Her big break came in April 1965 when she became an editorial writer with WDAF-TV, the first black to be employed by a Kansas City television station. Two years later she became an on-camera reporter concentrating on the city's educational system. Smith also reported on labor topics, including the development of the Kansas City Federation of Teachers. Ken Robinson, news director of WDAF-TV, said, "She was quite capable of getting any kind of story. She had that special quality of getting the human element into her story. That was her forte." Intelligent, even-handed coverage of controversial issues was her style.

*Lena Rivers Smith with engineer, Dave McKinstry.*

COURTESY WDAF-TV

But she was both a black and a woman. Black women entering the work force at that time were seldom warmly welcomed. Smith was no exception. She channeled the frustrations created by the treatment she had received during her life in a positive way by joining many civil rights groups and the Panel of American Women to promote harmony and understanding between races.

One of the best-known local public figures, Lena Rivers Smith died of a heart attack at her home, 4247 Bellefontaine Avenue, on November 18, 1968, and was buried at Blue Ridge Lawn Cemetery. Only 46 years old, she was one of the very few black television reporters in the Midwest. In her honor the Panel of American Women established the Lena Rivers Smith Scholarship Fund to encourage black youths to enter journalism.

# NELL SNEAD

FOR OVER 40 YEARS she was *The Kansas City Star*'s quick-witted fashion editor who covered the latest styles from Paris to Petticoat Lane, two English coronations, and the wedding of the Duke and Duchess of Windsor.

Nell Snead was born January 20, 1885, in Oakdale, Nebraska, but spent most of her youth in Takameh, a small town north of Omaha. After completing her college degree, she taught high school English in her hometown. While on a summer vacation, Snead applied for a job with *The Star* on a whim. She didn't know a soul at the paper but was hired for the summer on June 12, 1918. By September teaching was out and journalism was in.

At first she was assigned to the city desk, reporting on the Kansas legislature, but soon took over the woman's page. In accepting the position, Snead insisted that she be sent to New York City to study the current fashions. This was her first of many trips for the paper, an aspect of the job that she adored. Snead covered Paris openings at some of the most famous couturiers, including Dior, Balmain, Patou, and Chanel. She also expanded the parameters of her writing to produce accounts of cathedrals, museums, art galleries, people, and places. Her writing earned her the respect of readers and the admiration of her colleagues.

Excitement and danger were a part of her life. In 1957 she was a passenger on a plane en route to London when it crashed near Boulogne, France. "We were being served an excellent French meal when the plane fell." Miraculously she survived, and as she was hauled from the wreckage, she yelled, "I'm not dead!" Shortly afterward the plane burst into flames.

She had impeccable taste in clothing and her own assessment of its importance: "A woman without fashion sense is like an egg without salt." Her interests included Sevres china, costume books (in 1967 she donated 200 to the University of Missouri-Kansas City library), *Godey's Lady's Books*, and the writings of Keats.

When Snead joined the paper in 1918, she was one of just five women on the staff. But over the years there were 16 of "Nell's chicks" who were taught newspaper writing and received fashion and personal advice from the grande dame. John Colt, one of her editors said, "She's a free spirit . . . Miss Snead blazed trails for women's lib."

She did have one imperfection. Her penmanship and two-finger typing were terrible—both had to be transcribed by reporters assigned to the task. Bill Vaughan of "Starbeams" fame wrote that once he had been that designated reporter. "After she first made [the copy] illegible by her own corrections in

COURTESY CHARNO'S CREATIVE PORTRAITS

*Nell Snead*

purple ink, I was expected to translate it. When World War II broke out, I went willingly!"

Tributes and honors were numerous. In 1950 she was one of five women selected to receive the Women's National Press Club award for outstanding newspaper work. A year later Theta Sigma Phi, national honorary journalism society for women, named her an outstanding writer. She was a charter member of the Women's Council at the University of Missouri-Kansas City, which honored her in 1972 by creating the Nell Snead Fund. Snead was also one of the founders of the Belles of the American Royal (BOTAR). She was a life trustee at the Barstow School and was a member of the National Arts Foundation, Kansas City Philharmonic board, Friends of Art, Woman's City Club, and Women's Chamber of Commerce.

Snead retired as *The Star*'s fashion editor in 1961 after 43 years of work. She died January 5, 1978, at the age of 92. Daniel Mac-Morris, Kansas City painter and muralist, said in a tribute: "By nature she was totally without pretense. . . . She constantly enriched the lives of the rest of us around her, not only with her creative talent but also with her sincerity and simplicity. To many of us who have been privileged to be her friends through this past half century—she remains today our most unforgettable character."

# CLARA LEWIS STOVER

HER HUSBAND TOLD HER, "Someday I'll dress you in silks and diamonds and you'll have your own piano." Working together in the candy business they achieved these goals as well as many others they had not even dared to dream.

Clara Lewis was born in 1882 to Iowa farmers Lorenzo and Mary Ann Jenkins Lewis. One of four daughters, she attended elementary school in Oxford and borrowed money to attend high school at Iowa City Academy. While she was a student there, she met Russell Stover at a local confectionery and received a marriage proposal. They were married on June 17, 1911, in Iowa City when Russell was not quite 20 years old. With the innocence of youth, they went to Canada searching for their paradise. They found wind, cold, and mosquitoes. The couple returned to an apartment in Chicago where Russell sold candy.

Clara Stover, who had been taught candy making by her husband, made her first batch, and Russell quickly landed 16 accounts for Mrs. Stover's candy. Clara and one assistant cooked up 300 pounds of candy a week to satisfy the orders.

Russell's job took them to Omaha in 1921 where they revolutionized the ice cream market. Russell Stover created the Eskimo Pie, an ice cream bar coated with hard chocolate. It became a sensation with more than 20 million pies selling daily in early 1922. These happy days did not last long. There was fierce competition from other manufacturers flooding the market with similar products in order to get a share of the "pie." The Stovers regretted their decision to reject the $3 million offer made by William Wrigley to buy the rights, patents, and licenses for it.

The Stovers were involved in lawsuits to protect their product until the unexpected happened. Sales of Eskimo Pies began to fall off even during the summer months. Facing large losses instead of profits, the Stovers sold their company for $30,000 and returned to the basics: Mrs. Stover's candy.

With $2,500 and their Lincoln car they went to Denver, bought a bungalow, and began to put the pieces back together. The bungalow served several purposes. It was a home, a candy factory, and the inspiration for the company logo. The candy was from Mrs. Stover's Bungalow. Fresh every day was the slogan. Together they saw their business grow.

The first year was so successful that they began

*Clara Lewis Stover*

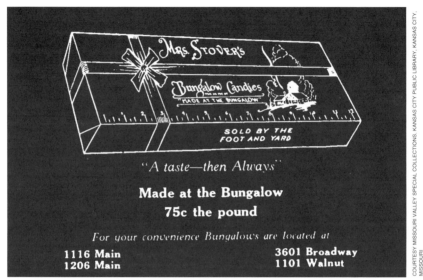

*Advertisement for Mrs. Stover's Bungalow Candies*

to look eastward to expand the market. Deciding that Kansas City was the best distribution point, they opened a factory in 1925 followed by two retail stores. Business was good, and they moved their national headquarters and their residence to Kansas City in 1931. Their retail outlets were designed to resemble bungalows, and by 1939 six stores in Kansas City had opened. (The store with a blue glass front at 1201 East Linwood Boulevard is still in existence.) The Eskimo Pie fiasco and the Depression kept them in debt until 1942, but the company grew stronger and larger with Russell Stover as president, Clara as vice-president.

Clara Stover joined the Women's Chamber of Commerce in 1931 and was active in the Business and Professional Women's Club, Soroptimist International of Kansas City, Woman's City Club, and the Advertising Club. With Phil A. Koury she wrote *The Life of Russell Stover: An American Success Story.* She preferred a simple life. "I don't play bridge or go to parties but am perfectly content just being at home evenings and Sundays."

In 1943 the Stovers purchased a mansion on a hill at 5805 Mission Drive where Clara remained until her death June 10, 1975. Her life reflects a close partnership with her husband in building a multimillion dollar business from a simple batch of homemade candy.

# GLADYS SWARTHOUT

HER STRIKING BEAUTY and rich mezzo-soprano voice took her from Deepwater, Missouri, to international fame in opera houses, radio, and movies during the 1930s and 1940s.

Gladys Swarthout was born on Christmas Day of 1904 in Deepwater. When she was only a few months old, Frank and Ruth Swarthout moved to 921 Cherry Street in Kansas City with their children. Gladys graduated from Central High School in 1920.

Her singing career began as a member of a church choir. Dressed in adult clothes with her dark curls pinned up, she auditioned for and was hired as a soloist at the tender age of 13. After high school, friends encouraged her to enroll at the Bush Conservatory of Music in Chicago where she stayed for three years. Gladys Swarthout then went on a concert tour with her sister Roma, the one who insisted that Gladys become an opera star. Roma accompanied her sister on the piano, sang duets with her, and served one additional function: keeping Gladys away from boys and vice versa.

In 1924 friends set up an audition with Cleofonte Campanini, director of the Chicago Civic Opera Company. Even though Swarthout lacked an operatic role in her repertoire, Campanini hired her. In just a few months she mastered 23 complete roles. Three years later she joined the Ravinia Opera Company in Chicago. She made her radio debut on WDAF, which was owned by *The Kansas City Star*, in 1927.

The Metropolitan Opera Company of New York City hired Swarthout in 1929. Her debut came that same year in *La Gioconda* as La Cieca, the blind mother. She performed in 25 other operas for the Met but was best known for her portrayal of the seductive Carmen. Swarthout enjoyed a successful career with the Met until she left in 1945.

While working at the Met during the 1930s, she was discovered by Hollywood. Famous, glamorous, and recognized for her acting ability, she was signed by Paramount Studios. Her films, including *Rose of the Rancho, Champagne Waltz,* and *Romance in the Dark*, did not prove to be box office sensations.

In 1950 she sang the role of Carmen in the first opera staged exclusively for television. Swarthout also went on concert tours and appeared regularly on radio on such programs as "Camel Caravan," the "Ford Symphony," and the "Prudential Family Hour."

Twice widowed, her first husband, Harry Richmond Kern, died in 1931, her second, baritone Frank M. Chapman, Jr., in 1966.

Swarthout made many appearances in Kansas City with the Philharmonic Orchestra. Her program was never restricted to opera but always included selections from Bizet's *Carmen*. Her fame in opera, radio, and motion pictures drew large hometown crowds. Her uncle, Dr. Donald M. Swarthout, was dean of the fine arts department of the University of Kansas.

She retired for health reasons in 1956 and died July 7, 1969, at her Italian villa near Florence. The little girl from Deepwater had grown up to become a famous mezzo-soprano, movie star, radio personality, and member of the best-dressed list.

*Gladys Swarthout with her husband, Frank M. Chapman, Jr. She often appeared on best-dressed lists.*

# VELMA WEST SYKES

URING A 60-YEAR career she wrote newspaper columns, hosted a radio show, reviewed books, edited a magazine, and wrote plays and poetry.

Velma West was born on July 24, 1892, in Kincaid, Kansas, the daughter of L.J. and Alice West. When she was ten years old, the family moved to Garnett, Kansas. Velma West was determined to be a journalist. Instead she married a journalist, George Beaumont Sykes, assignment editor of *The Kansas City Star*, who encouraged her to write contributions to the "Starbeams" column of the paper. "I had five daughters," Velma Sykes said, "so at first I worked at home," but later with more free time her writing career became established.

From 1936 to 1939 she wrote "The Chaperone," an advice column for *The Star*. Her articles, book reviews, and poetry were published not only in the newspaper but also in *Scientific Monthly, Kansas Magazine, Farm Journal,* and *The Saturday Evening Post*. She was an editor for *Capper's Farmer* and *The Household Magazine*.

One of the women pioneers in radio, Sykes wrote and directed her own plays on "Lady of the House" for Sears, Roebuck and Co. on KMBC. On "The Gentle Reader" she read her book reviews and poetry on WDAF.

After the death of her husband in 1941, she joined the staff of *Boxoffice*, the film industry magazine. For 25 years she served as associate editor. She was also chairman of its National

COURTESY BONNIE SYKES SULLIVAN

*Velma West Sykes*

Screen Council made up of 400 motion picture editors, radio commentators, members of educational organizations, exhibitor groups, and fan clubs. The council designated the films most suitable for family viewing. Sykes said near the end of her career, "I have enjoyed my work with the film industry. But I enjoyed it more, I'll admit, when there were more suitable family films." She retired when she was 77.

She was president of the Missouri Writers' Guild and the Kansas Poetry Society and was a charter member of The Diversifiers, a poetry club. Theta Sigma Phi honored her many writing achievements in 1970 with the Matrix Award for creative journalism.

Velma West Sykes, poet, writer, editor, and radio hostess died January 25, 1976, at the age of 83 shortly after her last article appeared in *The New England Galaxy* Magazine.

# MARION NEVADA TALLEY

*Marion Nevada Talley*

SHE BLAZED ACROSS the opera world with a meteoric career. "I felt I accomplished what was expected of me in music and even though I was very young it was better to exit gracefully than gradually to fade out," said Marion Nevada Talley.

She was born December 20, 1906, in Nevada, Missouri, to Charles and Helen Talley. Her father, a telegraph operator for the Missouri Pacific Railroad, moved his family to an apartment in Kansas City

at 1308 East Eighth Street when Marion was six months old.
By the time she was 12 she was singing in church choirs. Minna
K. Powell, music critic of *The Kansas City Star,* heard Talley sing and
was so impressed that she arranged an audition with Madame
Amelita Galli-Curci, famed Italian opera singer. "This child," Galli-
Curci said, "has a great gift. She must go to Chicago or New York
for study." But, Talley's family could not finance any vocal training,
so the idea was dropped. A few years later Madame Ernestine Schumann-Heink, world-acclaimed contralto, observed that, "This child
has a voice that will guarantee her a great future."

With the endorsement of two of the world's leading singers,
Minna K. Powell, Jacob A. Harzfeld, and John T. Harding rallied a
number of local music lovers to sponsor a fund-raising concert on
October 17, 1922. Over $10,000 was raised. Using this money, Tal-
ley went to New York with her mother and sister.

She studied with Frank LaForge and Salvatore Avitabile, noted
vocal coaches. Urged to train in Europe, Talley gave two concerts in
Kansas City that raised $13,000, thus enabling her to study in Italy.
She again was accompanied by her mother and sister.

Marion Talley made her debut with the Metropolitan Opera
Company on February 17, 1926, as Gilda in *Rigoletto.* She was just
19 years old. A specially chartered train carrying 200 of her Kansas
City fans generated so much advance publicity that over 10,000
curious New Yorkers waited for her to enter the opera house on
opening night. She made opera history during her debut. There
were 30 curtain calls for the new sensation. Newswriters hinted
that Talley was the world's greatest singer, an American nightingale.
Only Caruso had aroused so much excitement. Critics were not so
sure. "News editors," wrote one critic, "ran over the music critics."
Some negative comments about her voice did appear, but her popu-
larity was phenomenal.

For four seasons she sang coloratura roles with the Met.
Between opera seasons she toured the country in concerts that
earned about $300,000. Then at the age of 23 she announced her
retirement. She said that she had made enough money to be financially secure for life. Her last performance was in Cleveland in May
1929 in *Lucia di Lammermoor.*

Talley began performing on radio in 1931. But, her voice had
changed. Minna K. Powell wrote, "It is difficult for anyone who

heard her in 1922 to listen to the Talley voice today without a certain prejudice in favor of the free and lovely singing of the earlier period." She joined the Chicago Opera Company in 1934, but the magic was gone and she left.

Talley next tried Hollywood and signed a contract with Republic Pictures. Again, she moved on. She had recording contracts and made occasional radio appearances. In 1936 she was a regular on "Music All America Loves," a weekly program heard on WDAF. She retired again.

Two marriages and two divorces left her with a daughter. All the Talley women, Marion, her mother, her sister, and one daughter, settled in Beverly Hills, California. Marion Nevada Talley, Kansas City's opera star, radio performer, and movie actress, died there in obscurity on January 3, 1983.

# FANNIE BROWN TAYLOR

W HO AND WHAT could make the city's most influential newspaper change one of its established policies that resulted in a

*Fannie Brown Taylor*

loss of revenue? Fannie Brown Taylor, president of the Kansas City chapter of Women's Christian Temperance Union (WCTU), and a parade did just that.

Fannie Louise Brown was born October 1, 1844, in Carroll County, Missouri, the daughter of Oscar and Malinda Jane Brown. Her childhood was spent in Pleasant Hill, home of a distillery and several saloons, but she lived in a home where total abstinence was practiced.

When she was 12 years old, Fannie Brown attended a revival

meeting conducted by Francis Murphy, a great supporter of Prohibition. Moved by the message, Fannie signed the Murphy pledge and received a strip of blue ribbon that symbolized total abstinence.

At 17 she was a widow with a small child. Even though at that time the expectations of widowhood included retirement from public activities, Fannie Brown found it necessary to do the opposite. She turned to the WCTU and assisted the state president in organizing a local chapter. She was made the treasurer, and her life's course was determined.

Marriage to John L. Taylor on October 16, 1880, brought her to Kansas City where she continued her work with the WCTU. Under her leadership as president of the federated unions four original unions grew to 15, and membership increased from 128 to 1,247. Fannie Brown Taylor excelled as an organizer, lecturer, and writer. Her message to schools, churches, and clubs was that alcohol was evil. She wrote newspaper articles supporting Prohibition and composed several "dry" songs. Words were her weapons.

As part of the organization's first statewide campaign endorsing Prohibition in 1910, Fannie Taylor directed a WCTU parade led by R.A. Long, well-known businessman and civic leader. Members of the WCTU, clergy, and other supporters marched through the Fifteenth Street saloon district and north on Grand Avenue. Brewers and saloon owners did all they could to break up the parade: brewery wagons wound in and out, and bottles and stones were thrown at parade participants, a number of whom were wounded.

Watching from the window of his office at Eleventh Street and Grand Avenue was William Rockhill Nelson, owner of *The Kansas City Star*, who was incensed at what he saw. He called the police, and that evening the paper strongly denounced the violence. Nelson decided that the newspaper would no longer accept liquor advertisements even though it meant a significant loss of revenue. Fannie Taylor was a force to be reckoned with.

She announced her retirement from WCTU in 1926 after 66 years as a member, 33 of which were as an officer, predicting that Prohibition would return "because the lawlessness of the liquor traffic and the constant violation of all the laws concerning liquor enforcement" would inspire the public to demand its reinstatement. She died on November 1, 1928.

# LEONA POUNCEY THURMAN

F OR DECADES EIGHTEENTH and Vine has been known as the home of Kansas City jazz. In that area jazz clubs and other black-

owned businesses flourished during Prohibition. But, decay soon set in. By the late 1970s efforts to revitalize the area began; one of the most avid champions was Leona Pouncey Thurman.

She was born July 1, 1911, in Russellville, Arkansas, one of two children of James and Walsae Hendrix. After attending Henderson Business College in Memphis, she traveled to Kansas City in 1931 and became an accomplished secretary for James D. Pouncey, an attorney whom she married in 1937. She was active in the black community.

Wanting more education, she entered Lincoln University in Jefferson City and graduated in 1947. Her experience in her husband's office furthered her interest in law. After his death, Leona Pouncey received

*Leona Pouncey Thurman in front of her office on East 18th Street.*

COURTESY MISSOURI VALLEY SPECIAL COLLECTIONS, KANSAS CITY PUBLIC LIBRARY, KANSAS CITY, MISSOURI

a law degree from Howard University in 1949 and became the first black woman to practice law in Kansas City. She stated that, "I encountered a lack of cooperation of black male attorneys. None of them cooperated with me or advised me or took me and introduced me to the court. I had to do that on my own." She worked as an attorney for over 34 years.

In 1957 she married Dr. A. Odell Thurman, who retired in 1979 as the director of planning, research, and evaluation for Kansas City public schools.

Leona Pouncey Thurman served as the chairman of the women's division of the World Peace Through Law Center and was an active member of the International Federation of Women Lawyers (she was its representative to the United Nations for three years), National Association of Women Lawyers, and the local, state, and national bar associations. She received the C. Francis Stradford Award from the National Bar Association in 1960. She served as president of the Southwest Bar Association.

A lifelong Republican, Leona Pouncey Thurman was a member of the National Federation of Women's Republican Clubs, served on the executive committee of the Citizens Association, and in 1969 was appointed by President Richard M. Nixon to a blue ribbon defense panel.

She was a member of the League of Women Voters, Booklovers Club, Women's Chamber of Commerce, and the YWCA. Thurman served on the boards of directors of the National Coalition of 100 Black Women (and helped found a local chapter), Greater Kansas City Chapter of the American Red Cross, Mid-Continent Council of Girl Scouts of America, and the Carver Neighborhood Center.

Although she could have practiced law anywhere, she remained in the inner city with an office at 1505 East Eighteenth Street. She worked vigorously to develop an outdoor amphitheater in the mini-park she owned on the northeast corner of Eighteenth Street and The Paseo. She said, "What better place to hold a jazz concert?" Her efforts to restore the Eighteenth and Vine area as a jazz center gave her much pleasure.

Leona Pouncey Thurman, the first black woman to practice law in Kansas City, died at her home on May 1, 1985, and was buried in Forest Hill Cemetery.

# MARY HARMON WEEKS

W HEN SHE BEGAN her teaching career at the age of 17, she had to promise W.G. Pratt, principal of Central High School, that she would keep her age a secret since she was younger than many of her students.

Tragedy struck early in the life of Mary Harmon, born April 22, 1851, in Warren, Ohio. When her father, a captain of a volunteer company, died in the Civil War, she was just nine years old. Mary learned of his death by overhearing neighbors discussing it, but the child kept the news a secret from her seriously ill mother for a few days to allow her time to recover. Seven years later, Mrs. Harmon and her children moved to Kansas City, and Mary was enrolled in high school at St. Teresa's Academy at Twelfth and Washington streets. She earned her teaching certificate in 1868.

The concept of offering a high school education was quite controversial when Central High School opened in 1867. Many

*Mary Harmon Weeks*

COURTESY © THE KANSAS CITY STAR COMPANY

believed it was a needless extravagance and a waste of taxpayers' money that just pampered children. It was in this atmosphere that Mary Harmon became one of the two teachers on staff. Among her students were Dr. Burris A. Jenkins, Fred Wolferman, and Frank C. Wornall. She taught nine subjects, but later her teaching load was reduced to mathematics and English. When she retired, she had completed 17 years as a member of the Central High School faculty.

In 1882 she married

Edwin Ruthven Weeks and had a daughter, Ruth Mary (who for many years headed the English Department at Paseo High School and was a nationally known author). J.V.C. Barnes, president of the board of education, persuaded Mary Harmon Weeks to return to teaching for a year so that his daughter could study algebra and geometry with her.

An author as well as an educator, she compiled and edited an eight-volume series entitled *Parents and Their Problems and Child Welfare in Home, School, Church and State* in 1914. One hundred and sixty-four authors, including Woodrow Wilson, Theodore Roosevelt, and Weeks herself, were featured in the series. The work was underwritten by the National Council of Mothers and the Parent-Teacher Association. Much of the material had appeared in the "Club Column" of *The Kansas City Star*.

Her accomplishments were extraordinary. In 1889, the year she placed her daughter in the city's first kindergarten, she organized a mothers' union, a group of mothers of children in the class. Weeks began a three-year campaign for establishing kindergartens in all the city's public schools that resulted in school board approval in 1894.

In the 1890s Weeks was one of the founders of the National Congress of Mothers and the Parent-Teacher Association. She organized the first PTA in Missouri. Her commitment was lifelong; she traveled to the PTA national convention in Richmond by herself when she was 86. Mary Harmon Weeks was also active in the Kansas City Art Institute and School of Design.

Weeks joined in the founding of several women's clubs, including the '81 Club, Tuesday Morning Study Club, Bancroft Club, and Kansas City Athenaeum.

She strongly supported preschool education and organized the first preschool circle in Missouri. She stated that, "I consider preschool work and instruction the most important phase of education. Because it is the foundation, because it is the building up of the physical, mental, and spiritual being of the child at his most responsive age. Everything that comes after rests on that foundation." Mary Harmon Weeks School at 4201 Indiana was named in her honor in recognition of her contributions to education in Kansas City.

A non-traditionalist with fresh ideas and innovative teaching methods, Mary Harmon Weeks died at her home, 3408 Harrison Street, on May 24, 1940.

# CARRIE WESTLAKE WHITNEY

S HE WAS THE MOTHER of Kansas City's public library system. Carrie Westlake was born on a plantation in Virginia to Wellington and Helen Westlake. After her family moved to Missouri, she received her education in private schools in St. Louis.

She took charge of the first circulating library in Kansas City at Eighth and Main streets in 1881. Although there were fewer than 1,000 volumes, Westlake began encouraging the school board and James M. Greenwood, superintendent of schools, to find money for the purchase of additional books. In 1883 and again in 1885 city tax money was approved to build the collection. In 1885 she married James Steele Whitney, a newspaperman who died five years later.

Under Carrie Whitney's direction the library so increased in size, services, and readers that the law was amended in 1889 permitting the board of education authority to erect buildings for public library use. When the new building located near the corner of Eighth and Oak streets was occupied, Whitney recommended that the $2 per year user fee be discontinued and the library stacks be opened for public use. Her suggestions were approved. Once again a growth spurt occurred necessitating the construction of a new library at Ninth and Locust streets in 1898.

First and foremost she believed that children must be encouraged to read. She was devoted to

*Carrie Westlake Whitney*

COURTESY MISSOURI VALLEY SPECIAL COLLECTIONS, KANSAS CITY PUBLIC LIBRARY, KANSAS CITY, MISSOURI

this concept and installed a special children's room with books just for them in the library. It was arranged and furnished with young readers in mind.

She also wrote prose and poetry for children. In 1909 she composed a Christmas greeting to the children of Kansas City which Sir Carl Busch put to music. Her works were frequently published; a constant theme was the importance of reading. Whitney also wrote *Kansas City, Missouri: Its History and Its People*, a three-volume work covering events from 1808 to 1908. Rare pictures and illustrations depicting the growth of the city appeared in the history. Two of the volumes were biographical sketches of prominent citizens.

After serving 29 years as head of the library, Whitney was removed from the position by a resolution adopted by the board of education. Purd B. Wright was appointed in her place. It was stated that the reason for the change was that a man should occupy the position. She became assistant librarian, but on September 5, 1912, she lost that job. Whitney had built the library to over 100,000 volumes during her tenure.

She remained active in the American Library Association, the Missouri Branch of the American Folklore Society, and Missouri Historical Society.

Carrie Westlake Whitney, mother of Kansas City's public libraries, died on April 8, 1934, and was buried in Forest Hill Cemetery.

# BRENDA PAULETTE WILLIAMS

S HE WAS MUCH MORE than just a pretty face on the local news. Brenda Williams was a role model for aspiring broadcast journalists, especially black women.

She was born in St. Louis on July 7, 1946, the daughter of Herman and Hattie Williams. After graduating from Beaumont High School, she received a B.S. degree from the University of Ohio at Athens in 1969. Williams did graduate work in journalism there and at the University of Missouri-Columbia.

Her first job was with a St. Louis radio station as a newscaster and talk show host, followed by four years as a reporter on television before coming to Kansas City in 1977 as a reporter on KMBC-TV, Channel 9. By 1980 she had been promoted to the weekend anchor slot. Although popular with viewers, she was demoted to reporter. In August 1981 Christine Craft, a weekday co-anchor at the station, refused to accept a demotion to reporter and left the station claiming she was a victim of sexism. Williams was offered and accepted Craft's former job and signed a three-year contract. Brenda Williams became Kansas City's first black weekday anchorwoman. In accepting the position, she was well aware of the expectations and pressures that awaited her. By all accounts she handled the position in a professional manner.

At the end of her contract, she was offered a raise with the proviso that she would have to play the role of second banana to the male anchor. Unable to accept this change in terms, Williams filed a race and sex discrimination complaint with the Equal Employment Opportunity Commission and left the station. Coming to an agreement with the Hearst Corporation, owner of the station, she dropped the complaint and returned to work. She resigned in 1985.

For several years Williams worked in real estate, public relations, and as a financial consultant. Poor health forced her to return to St. Louis where she died of cancer at the age of 43 on January 17, 1989. Burial was in St. Peter's Cemetery in St. Louis.

*Brenda Paulette Williams*

The Brenda P. Williams Foundation was established to assist minority students interested in pursuing journalism careers. The first scholarship was awarded in 1991.

# HAZEL BROWNE WILLIAMS

S HE WAS THE FIRST black fulltime professor at the University of Kansas City (later the University of Missouri-Kansas City). After serving as a member of the faculty for 18 years, in 1976 Hazel Browne Williams was accorded emeritus status, the first black person to be so honored.

A native Kansas Citian, Hazel Browne was born February 9, 1907, to John and Effie Moten Browne. An only child, she attended a Kansas City elementary school and in 1923 graduated from Lincoln High School. She showed her mettle in her senior year when she challenged and broke tradition by serving as the first woman sponsor major of the Lincoln High School Reserve Officers' Training Corps (ROTC).

Browne did not have a burning desire to become a teacher, but as a black woman in the 1920s she could either study to become a teacher or a librarian. Choosing the former, she entered the University of Kansas (the University of Missouri prohibited admission of blacks) in 1923 and graduated in 1927 with an academic record so distinguished that she was elected to Phi Beta Kappa. "When I was elected, *The Star* sent a reporter to interview me. When the reporter saw I was black, he refused to do the interview." Life on the Lawrence campus was not easy. Browne felt that black students were all but ignored by the faculty and administration. She chose to remain at the university and earned her master's degree in English in 1929.

Browne began her teaching career in 1932 as an assistant professor of English at Louisville Municipal College, a liberal arts school for blacks that was a branch of the University of Louisville. Although her university degrees were in English, her minor was in German. Browne shifted to teaching German and established a department of German. She left Louisville to attend Columbia Uni-

*Dr. Hazel Browne Williams*

versity, from which she received a master's degree in guidance and counseling. From 1948 through 1951 she was an instructor at New York University where she received her Ph.D. in 1953. Two years later, utilizing her skills in German, she received a Fulbright teaching appointment in Vienna where she taught English and American culture.

Earlier in her career she had married Claude Williams, a principal of Leeds Junior High School. He died in 1937.

In 1958 Dr. Hazel Browne Williams came to the University of Kansas City as an associate professor on the faculty of the school of education and became a full professor in secondary education in 1960. She retired in 1976 to work on a book dealing with the black role in American education. "As far back as the 1900s there has been black participation in educating Americans. They were superintendents. There have always been some very fine teachers of black people, but there has always been the policy of downgrading whatever we were doing. I want this book to bring some perspective to the role blacks have played educating black and white Americans." Ill health prevented Williams from completing the book.

Her professional and community affiliations were numerous, including the National Council of Teachers of English, International Society for General Semantics, Modern Language Association, Missouri State Teachers Association, and the American Association of University Professors. She participated in many community organizations, such as the Carver Neighborhood Center, Mattie Rhodes Center, YWCA, and NAACP.

Williams was listed in *Who's Who Among American Women* and *Who's Who Among Black Americans*. In 1977 she received the Thomas Jefferson Award for excellence in teaching from the University of Missouri.

Dr. Hazel Browne Williams died July 7, 1986, and was buried in Forest Hill Cemetery. A former dean of the UMKC School of Education said, "Her contribution to history and education will be everlasting for she stimulated the imagination of students."

**KANSAS CITY WOMEN
OF INDEPENDENT MINDS**

was designed by Gene Funk,
edited by Barbara Funk,
digitally composed in Stempel Schneidler
and printed on
Weyerhaeuser Natural Cougar Opaque Vellum

by
The Lowell Press, Inc.
115 East 31st Street
P.O. Box 411877
Kansas City, Missouri 64141-1877